Praise for

MINITRENDS

How Innovators & Entrepreneurs Discover & Profit From Business & Technology Trends

An Eric Hoffer Business Book Award Winner. "The ability to capitalize on newly emerging business trends is the premise of this book. There are 'Minitrends' all around us, defined as those that 'promise to become significantly important within the next two to five years.' ... By reading this book, you will learn how to take hold of these opportunities, overcome common obstacles, and ultimately profit from Minitrends."

—The Eric Hoffer Project

ForeWord Reviews' Business Book of the Year Finalist. "Vanston has the ability to discuss minitrends conceptually, as well as describe specifically how the reader can discover and potentially profit from them. The author's enthusiasm for the subject is infectious, and readers looking for new business opportunities are likely to share that enthusiasm. This is a book that should inspire many readers to take action."

—*ForeWord Reviews*

A Dan Poynter's Global Business eBook Award Finalist.

—Global eBook Awards

"Vanston's company, Technology Futures, has been making predictions about technology and business trends since 1978. Here, he describes how individual entrepreneurs, as well as companies, can find and exploit "minitrends" ... small trends (not yet recognized by the public) that have the potential to grow. ... This title offers a new take on possible product development and investment avenues."

—*Library Journal*

"In *MINITRENDS*, Technology Futures Inc. chairman John Vanston has distilled insights and techniques developed over a highly successful 40-year career in technology forecasting into a 189-page do-it-yourself guide to the early identification of those emerging developments that eventually become the 'next big things.'"

—*The Futurist*

"This book spotlights specific 'minitrends' and trains people how to recognize them and take advantage of related job opportunities."

—*Yahoo News*

"For the individual who wants to improve their personal finances, this volume proceeds from the process of searching for a Minitrend to developing an exploitation scheme. In between is an exploration of nine attractive Minitrends, including ones that could be taken advantage of by larger companies, with the employee playing a key role in their pursuit."

—*Book News* (Annotation ©2011 Book News Inc. Portland, OR)

"*MINITRENDS* is one of the most important books for technology entrepreneurs written in the last decade. With diligent attention to processes and trends, it provides a specific set of factors that entrepreneurs should consider in order to maximize the opportunity for success in the marketplace."　—August E. Grant, Ph.D., Professor
University of South Carolina

"I'd recommend this book to anyone looking to find a niche to call their own when it comes to business opportunities."

—Thomas "Duffbert" Duff, *Duffbert's Random Musings*

"*MINITRENDS* is short, unpretentious, and easy to read. … Minitrend-spotting is an interesting idea, and I believe a valuable one. "

—John Peters, *Management Decision*

"As I go deeper into the chapters, the more I like the book! You have managed to hit the sweet spot of this fascinating concept of Minitrends. The book itself is a precious gem."

—Guy deManuel, President, Sigma
Dataserv Informática (Brazil)

"This book is packed with usable 'how to' information and real life examples about how to find Minitrends and take action to prosper from them. Delivered with a little humor, it goes beyond a reference book, pointing readers toward their own inner thoughts and frustrations and on to countless information sources. I'm very excited about this book. *MINITRENDS* will definitely be used as a conversation piece, but that will only be the beginning."

—Terry B. Newman, Assistant Vice President, Graduate
School, The University of Texas at Austin

"I have read a lot of business books, but *MINITRENDS* is definitely unique, which is refreshing. It's also very timely given the state of the economy and the fact that businesses are having to redefine themselves if they are to stay afloat. It is clear that Dr. Vanston has a wealth of knowledge on the subject."

—Laura Alter, Search Engine Optimization Expert, All Web Leads, Inc.

"In *MINITRENDS* Dr. Vanston brings a systematic and analytical approach to the identification and exploitation of technological breakthroughs. He uses a wealth of 'real-world' examples to show the advantages, both personal and professional, of such an approach."

—Richard Drury, BGen, USAF (ret), Sr. Lecturer & Associate Chairman (ret), Department of Aerospace Engineering & Engineering Mechanics, The University of Texas at Austin

"Attempting to predict the future is always a dicey proposition, but John Vanston has used his powerful, common-sense approach to identify what can only be described as the inevitable. The book stimulated me to think of a few Minitrends of my own."

—Howard Smallowitz, Project Manager, IBM

"Starting with the advantages of high education in engineering and personal work in technology, John Vanston has over the years led seminar sessions with thousands of experienced and well-supported managers and technical staffers in exploring and exchanging views and experiences on how to discover and exploit fresh new business opportunities. With the Minitrends Concept he shares what he has learned from this extraordinarily rich input. This makes *MINITRENDS* in my view, not a cookbook or short list of catchy topics, but rather a rich collection of ways to prod and refresh creative thinking to achieve future technological innovation."

—Karl Vesper, Ph.D., Kent R. Hance Distinguished Visiting Regents Chair in Entrepreneurship, Texas Tech University

"*MINITRENDS* contains an arsenal of resources and frameworks for discovering and exploiting new market directions. It is dense with relevant examples and details, yet is enjoyable and compelling reading. Looking back on all the business books I've read, it is sincerely one of the most refreshingly honest and direct pieces. There is so much packed into so few pages that finishing a book and knowing you can go out and take action on what you've read is unique in my experience."

—Brook Capps, Product Line Manager Fortune 50 Computer Manufacturer

"*MINITRENDS* is a wonderful book to help people turn on their inner investor ear. As a banker, I see this book as a useful tool that teaches individuals how to identify and analyze trends that are all around. This can help individuals gain more wealth, resulting in more capital to live better lives."

—Tanisha Walter, Vice President, Wealth
Management Banker, Bank of America

"In this readable, well-organized discourse, Dr. Vanston masterfully guides the reader from the stage of passively experiencing current events to a stage that enables one to discern actively nuances and implications within business and social contexts that can signify new trends. We need more such expert guidance into the development of the higher order cognitive skills of creativity, interpretation, and judgment in order to prepare our young people for the decade ahead."

—Henry Baird, Associate Dean, ITT Technical Institute, Seattle

"As the world goes through this period of major change that only happens every 100 years or so, we find that those things that 'always worked' no longer do. *MINITRENDS* is timely in exposing and explaining the gold mine of new opportunities that exist for us. The book comes along at just the right time to help business and government leaders rapidly grasp the mind-boggling technology developments, put them in language that can be understood, and convert them into practical applications for a highly competitive marketplace."

—Ervin (Butch) Ackman, Organization Change
Management, RWD Technologies

"Having spent 25 years as an information professional, I have watched the Internet and the Web thoroughly transform the information industry and the information seeking and managing behaviors of end-users. In this book Dr. Vanston outlines his approach for identifying the signs that indicate Minitrends in your own environment. He then provides valuable tools that anyone can use to interpret them and then profit from them."

—Mark McFarland, Associate Director for Digital
Initiatives, The University of Texas at Austin
and Co-Director of the Digital Library

"*MINITRENDS* made me think in ways that I had previously not considered. Reading the book provided me with a catalyst to cut through the brush and open additional pathways of opportunity."

—Roger Storer, Investor/Entrepreneur

"I really enjoyed this book and could not put it down. *MINITRENDS* is a great source of practical advice for helping me find and act on ideas for creating new opportunities in all areas of my home and work life. I highly recommend it for anyone motivated to get more out of life."
—Tim Rotunda, System Software Engineer.
Fortune 50 Technology Company

"*MINITRENDS* is the best guidebook I've found for today's technology marketplace. We're in a time of tumultuous change and this book is full of practical tools to help marketers figure out which changes are actually points on a trend line, which trends are pointing to business opportunities, and which opportunities are the most promising. This is essential stuff for marketers, entrepreneurs, analysts, and anyone else interested in where business and technology are headed. I highly recommend it."
—Kermit L. Ross, President & Founder,
Millennium Marketing

"An important part of any business is ensuring product offerings remain aligned with ever-changing market conditions. The Minitrends concept enables colleges to better anticipate new market conditions and adapt their product offerings for increased student success after the classroom."
—Michael Bettersworth, Associate Vice Chancellor for Technology Advancement, Texas State Technical College

"*MINITRENDS* is an excellent book that I am confident will be very useful to its readers. I, personally, found the sections of the book that included plentiful examples to be most valuable."
—Mark Kapner, Strategic Planning & Enterprise
Development, Austin Energy

"*MINITRENDS* offers a highly readable route through numerous examples of Minitrends presented in a structure that makes grasping the concepts both enjoyable and a rapid read. The very fact that Minitrends are likely to be overlooked offers huge opportunities for those wise enough to spot and capitalize on them. The path blazed is clear: assessment of value, searching, examples of small to large enterprise issues, and, finally, profiting from Minitrends. Wherever the reader is, there is a place for her or him in this book."
—Jim Bryce, Attorney at Law

"I heartily recommend *MINITRENDS* for anyone in marketing, sales, or any role related to business development. This book did not just provide me with food for thought. It provided a huge feast! I eagerly turned the pages as I discovered more great ideas and ways of thinking that could provide me with much material and inspiration in my own line of work."

—Todd W. Smith, Executive Consultant, Bradley-Morris, Inc.

"Dr. Vanston has for years been a leading professional in the art and practice of technology forecasting. Now, with his daughter Carrie, he has pushed the art even further with their new book, *MINITRENDS*. For both individuals and organizations of all types, I recommend it as a practical way to improve both foresight and effectiveness."

—Oliver Markley, Ph.D., Professor Emeritus of Studies of the Future, University of Houston, Clear Lake, and Principal, InwardBoundVisioning.com

"Dr. Vanston's concise framework for exploiting emerging trends takes trend spotting from merely interesting social conversation, to valuable business opportunities and beyond. I found *MINITRENDS* to be a practical 'how to' guide to discovering, analyzing, and benefiting from emerging trends applicable to my industry and market. Packed with specific Minitrend examples from social media, technology, telecommunications, and the like, this book serves as a valuable resource for any home business, entrepreneur, or corporate executive."

—Alfredo Herrera, Owner, Levity Properties, and Supply Chain Management, U.S. Semiconductor Company

"Almost 30 years ago, I read with great interest Naisbitt's book *Megatrends*. *MINITRENDS* differs from *Megatrends* in that it provides instructions that have allowed me to personalize my own data mining procedures so that I can solve my own problems. The book is so packed with sources of information, it is hard to understand how Dr. Vanston got it all done. He must have a staff of hundreds, jars full of NoDoz, and cots in the office."

—Dayle Baldauf, Baldauf & Associates Real Estate

Other Publications Authored or Co-Authored by John H. Vanston, Ph.D.

Technology Forecasting: An Aid to Effective Technology Management

Introduction to Technology Market Forecasting

Mechatronics: A Technology Forecast

Home Technology Integration: A Technology Forecast

Biotechnology: A Technology Forecast

Emerging Technology Programs: ADM, Hybrids, Computer Forensics, and MEMS

Homeland Security: A Technology Forecast

Fuel Cells: A Technology Forecast

Nanotechnology: A Technology Forecast

Innovate! Straight Path to Quality, Customer Delight, and Competitive Advantage

Industrial Electrification in the Information Age

Principles for Electric Power Policy

MINITRENDS

How Innovators & Entrepreneurs Discover & Profit From Business & Technology Trends

Between Megatrends & Microtrends Lie MINITRENDS: Emerging Business Opportunities in the New Economy

By John H. Vanston, Ph.D.

with Carrie Vanston

Published by
TECHNOLOGY FUTURES INC.

MINITRENDS

How Innovators & Entrepreneurs Discover & Profit From Business & Technology Trends

By John H. Vanston, Ph.D., with Carrie Vanston
Creative Director: Helen Mary V. Marek
Technology Futures, Inc.

Printed in the United States of America.

Cover design and interior photo editing by Helen Mary V. Marek.
Cover background and section photos © 2010
Photos.com & Clipart.com, divisions of Getty Images.

Follow Minitrends Activities at
www.minitrends.com

ISBN: 978-1-884154-36-2 (pbk)
ISBN: 978-1-884154-37-9 (ePDF)
ISBN: 978-1-884154-38-6 (ePUB)

Published by

TECHNOLOGY FUTURES INC.

13740 Research Blvd, Suite C-1, Austin, Texas 78750-1859
(512) 258-8898 • (800) TEK-FUTR [835-3887]
info@tfi.com • www.tfi.com

Library of Congress Cataloging-in-Publication Data:
Vanston, John H.
MINITRENDS: How Innovators & Entrepreneurs Discover & Profit From Business & Technology Trends / John H. Vanston with Carrie Vanston
xxii, 190 p.; ill. 23 cm; includes index
1. Success in business. 2. Technological innovations. 3. Self-realization
Classification: HF5386.V267 2010
Control no. 2011420452
ISBN: 978-1-884154-36-2

Table of Contents

Part V: Becoming a Minitrends Master

Acknowledgments

If I were to list all of the people who have contributed to the development of this book, the list would probably be longer than the book itself. Therefore, I can only mention a small number of the contributors and apologize to those who have been left out.

The individuals involved can be characterized into two general groups—those who were directly involved in the preparation of the book and those with whom I have worked over the last few decades and who have provided me with the experiences on which the book is based.

Foremost in the first category are my two daughters, Carrie Vanston and Helen Mary Marek, both members of the Technology Futures, Inc. (TFI) team. Carrie worked with me as collaborator on the overall content, structure, and narrative of the book. Helen Mary was tireless in designing the layout, graphic, and cover material, as well as working on the editing and production. My son, Larry Vanston, President of TFI, encouraged me to write the book and put the resources of the company at my disposal during the writing and publication processes.

Lee Kuck also assisted in the editing process and helped to bring life to my prose, and Debra Robison, who has been a friend and TFI colleague for many years, helped format a host of loose papers into a real book.

John Harrison, David Armistead, Leslie Jarmon, Kavita Patek, Oliver Markley, Mark Kapner, and Dave Evans took time from their busy schedules to provide special insights on the Minitrends discussed in the book. Howard Smallowitz, Terry Newman, Brian Massey, Michael Bettersworth, Jim Bryce, and Henry Baird were kind enough to review a prepublication copy of the book and make useful comments.

I would particularly like to express my appreciation to my friends, Chuck and Jeanne Graves, who reviewed the book in great detail and who indicate a special understanding of the objectives of the *MINITRENDS* book in its Foreword.

The colleagues with whom I have worked represent a wide variety of talents, skills, and personalities. Three of my colleagues at the University of Texas at Austin who provided me with excellent ideas and insights were Lynn Draper, Herb Woodson, and Phil Schmidt. Each of these individuals is talented, imaginative, and just plain nice.

Since the Minitrends book is based in large measure on information, ideas, and insights that I have gained during my work at Technology Futures, Inc., I must acknowledge the contributions of some of my TFI colleagues through the years. First and foremost, I would like to express my appreciation and admiration for Jim Bright and Ralph Lenz. Jim was the person who first got me interested in technology forecasting, provided solid guidance, and played a major role in the start and continued success of TFI. Ralph has been one of my closest friends for many, many years. He was one of the first people to realize that formal techniques could be used to project advances in technology. Ralph and I have shared many great adventures, personal and professional—and more than a few scotches through the years.

Donna Prestwood, David Frederick, and Patti Holstrom were with TFI from the beginning and played major roles in our early successes. Over the years, many others joined the company and added to my intellectual growth and the joy of my work. A few who deserve special mention are Peter Zandan, Christopher Avery, Lisa Sullivan, Peter Nance, Samia El-Badry, Bill Kennedy, Bruce Kravitz, Laurel Anderson, Kirsten Palmbo, Julia Marsh Klepac, Ray Hodges, Paul Schumann, Tim Bigham, Claudia Crowley, Nancy Lux, Alvin Tong, George Alberts, David Smith, Bill Kleinebecker, and Henry Elliott. Each of these individuals played a special role in TFI operations.

I would also like to thank all of the non-TFI people with whom I have worked and from whom I have learned over the last three decades. These include, among many others, David Snyder, Margaret Lehning, George Murray, Guy deManuel, Joe Coates, Karl Vesper, Bob Spears, Rene Zentner, John Wood, Tom Sparrow, Jay Zarnikau, and Michael Bettersworth.

In addition, I would like to express Carrie's and my appreciation to our publicist, Steve O'Keefe of SixEstate Communications, for his assistance in the planning and execution of our promotional program, and to George Bounacos of Silver Beacon Marketing, for his assistance with our marketing efforts. Both have demonstrated great imagination and practical expertise during our coordinated efforts.

Finally, I must thank my beloved wife, Angela, for her understanding and support during the year-and-a-half in which I have been involved in writing this book. She has served as an adviser, a confidant, and an inspiration. This book is dedicated to her.

Foreword

Whether to improve your business, enhance your finances, or just to find greater personal satisfaction, there is no shortage of guidebooks. One problem with most "how to succeed" manuals, is that their work plans assume a ready and accessible supply of "good ideas" to exploit. The first lesson of Dr. John Vanston's new book, *MINITRENDS*, is to debunk that premise and propose a process for originating good ideas beforehand.

Abundant and concisely presented ideas for exploiting growth areas tumble over one another in this book guaranteed to whet your appetite to find new avenues to exploit in your business pursuits. As a reader, you may marvel at the many options the writer lays out. There's not a chapter without multiple channels for you to explore in-depth or glancingly, as you prefer.

Minitrends also demonstrates how you can glean those incipient "good ideas" or opportunities from an almost infinitely large set of options that others have not yet comprehended in any detail. Dr. Vanston teaches how to scope out a systematic and doable discovery path through diverse sources containing clues about changes just beginning to happen.

As opposed to Megatrends such as global warming, the rise of China, the convergence of telephones and computers, and the aging of the population, Minitrends are—one might say—the innumerable ripples within the sea swells of established ideas, with some of these ripples destined to be the genesis of waves. Or even tsunamis, like modern computing, whose current shape was imagined by very few 20 years ago. The challenge is how to survey the ripples within the larger body of established ideas, and how to find those with a tangible destiny that can be shaped into products or services.

Dr. Vanston has called upon his own 30 years as a technology forecasting expert to cite examples of projections that were correct to guide the reader through the process of selecting a Minitrend to explore. He is objective with practical advice to keep the reader from drowning in details or research. The author pulls together advice on melding personal relationships, professional organizations, a wealth of Web and academic sources, and specific examples to create a serious individual database with which to judge the wisdom of moving forward to exploit a Minitrend.

The book offers a balanced view of paths to take to discover the Minitrends most likely to succeed and advice on how to assess the risks and rewards within a given trend.

MINITRENDS is inspirational within a businesslike structure. It is well worth reading at any stage of a career.

Jeanne Graves, *Owner*
Research Communications

Charles E. Graves
Intellectual Property Attorney

Preface

The objective of this book is quite simple—to provide you, the reader, with information, insights, and suggestions that will materially improve your business situation, your financial standing, and your personal satisfaction. The basis for achieving these improvements is the identification, evaluation, and exploitation of "Minitrends."

Minitrends have the following characteristics:

- They are trends—technical, social, economic, regulatory, demographic, etc—that are just beginning to emerge.

- They have the potential to become significantly important in a reasonably short time, i.e., two to five years.

- They are either not recognized by the general public and most organizations or their potential importance is not appreciated.

Following the Minitrend concept outlined in this book, i.e., joining in the "Minitrend Adventure," gives you the opportunity to utilize and express your imagination, your perceptiveness, your originality, your logic, your innovative nature, and your basic good sense. Minitrend involvement also provides you a way to distinguish yourself from your colleagues and contemporaries.

The way that you can best utilize Minitrends depends on your position, your personality, and your objectives in life. If you are an individual or a member of a small group of individuals, you can use Minitrends to identify and evaluate new entrepreneurial business opportunities. If you are in a decision-making position in an existing small or medium-sized company, you can use Minitrends to promote significant changes in the product mix of the company or to identify means for significantly improving the operations of the organization. If you are an employee of a large company, you can use Minitrends to identify new business ventures for the company.

Once you commit yourself to the Minitrend Adventure, you will find yourself looking at the world in a totally different manner. When a new law is passed, a new business is launched, an important person makes an unexpected statement, or a new technical or scientific discovery is announced, you will find yourself searching for Minitrends embedded in this event. Moreover, on some level, you will begin to consider what business opportunities might result from the event.

As you continue on your Minitrend Adventure, you will identify an enormous number of interesting Minitrends. Analyzing these Minitrends, selecting the ones to exploit, and translating them into successful business applications can be interesting, rewarding, and just plain fun!

In this regard, we welcome reader interaction as explained in the reader letter at the end of this book and on our Minitrends website and blog at http://minitrends.com/blog/.

This book is organized into five parts.

In Part One: *The Value of Minitrends* (Chapter 1), I discuss how Minitrends can assist you and your organization to increase both the probability and extent of success. I give examples of people and organizations that have converted an awareness and appreciation of Minitrends into successful business opportunities, as well as examples of individuals and companies that have suffered because of failure to recognize emerging Minitrends.

In Part Two: *Uncovering Minitrends* (Chapters 2-3), I present techniques and strategies to assist you in identifying promising Minitrends and list a number of sources where you can find Minitrend-related information and insight.

In Part Three: *Some Attractive Minitrends* (Chapters 4-6), I analyze nine specific Minitrends. (Three of these Minitrends are particularly well-suited to individuals and small groups of individuals; three are particularly well-suited to small and medium-size companies; and three are particularly well-suited to large companies.) In each case, I discuss the background of the subject, current related trends, and potential business opportunities. Although I find each of these Minitrends to be both interesting and attractive, the main purpose of these chapters is to demonstrate how you can identify and analyze Minitrends of interest to you.

In Part Four: ***Prospering from Minitrends*** *(Chapters 7-9),* I discuss how you can translate promising Minitrends into business opportunities. I demonstrate how you can choose between different attractive Minitrends; how you can develop an effective Minitrend Exploitation Scheme (plan); and how you can convert that exploitation scheme into a successful business operation.

In Part Five: ***Becoming a Minitrends Master*** *(Chapter 10),* I summarize and correlate the ideas and insights presented in the previous nine chapters, and I indicate how searching for and exploiting Minitrends can become a natural part of your life.

At the end of each chapter of the book, I sum up what I believe to be the basic wisdom of that chapter. Although the subjects are presented one by one, in reality, the true value of the Minitrend concept is the melding of all of these individual subjects.

You will note that each heading page of Parts One through Five use "gem" analogies alluding to Minitrends. I like this metaphor because gems, like Minitrends, have inherent value, require effort to uncover, entail processing to achieve their full value, and can be very valuable to their discoverer.

The ideas and insights presented in this book are based on my thirty plus years of experience as founder, president, and current chairman of Technology Futures, Inc., an Austin, Texas consulting, research, and education firm; my years as a professor of nuclear engineering at the University of Texas at Austin; and service as an officer in the U.S. Army.

During these years I have supervised or participated in several hundred projects involving commercial organizations, government agencies, and academic institutions. These projects involved a wide range of services including technology forecasts and assessments, development of tactical and strategic plans, alternate scenario development and application, and trend analyses.

My collaborator, Carrie Vanston, brings a long history of marketing to the book, giving it a practical marketing and media savvy.

In this book I describe many of my personal experiences and those of people with whom I have worked. I believe that these experiences demonstrate how the principles and suggestions presented in the book apply in real life situations. This book is intended to be a "how to" volume and not a scholarly treatise.

ℭℬ ℰℴ

In his play, *Cato, The Tragedy,* Joseph Addison has the Roman Senator Cato declare to a fellow senator, "Tis not in mortals to command success, but we'll do more, Sempronius; we'll deserve it." Hopefully, if you utilize the percepts presented in this book, you will not only deserve success, but, more importantly, you will achieve it.

John H. Vanston, Ph.D.
Chairman, Technology Futures, Inc.

Part I: The Value of Minitrends

Precious gems can be very valuable to their owners, but attaining that value requires that each gem be discovered, its attributes analyzed, and its surfaces skillfully polished.

The first step in profiting from gems is recognizing the value of the individual stone. In a similar manner, benefiting from Minitrends requires that you first have an appreciation of their inherent value.

Chapter One

Importance of Minitrends

In 1982, John Naisbitt published the book *Megatrends*, describing ten overarching trends that would "define our society." Today, more than two decades later, many of those trends are still relevant: our transformation from an industrial society into an information society, from a national economy to a world economy, and from a representative democracy to a participative demography.

Naisbitt's insights sensitized us to the emergence of new Megatrends: the rise of China as a major and growing economic power, the convergence of computing and communications technologies, the movement from a Physics Age to a Biology Age, our increasing awareness of the impacts of climate change, increased government intervention into the financial arena, new long-term energy shortages, the aging of populations in many of the world's most prosperous nations, and they just keep coming.

Even though all of these Megatrends have important implications for individuals, companies, and governments throughout the world, they are generally well-recognized and understood. Therefore, these overarching Megatrends offer little competitive advantage to specific individuals or businesses. Yet buried in each of these Megatrends are less obvious emerging trends, which I choose to call "Minitrends."

Minitrends go hand-in-hand with Megatrends, but are harder to spot. Within the Megatrend of an aging population, for example, are the Minitrends of people remaining active in the workforce for longer periods of time and increasing movement of elderly individuals to smaller nursing centers. Within the Megatrend of convergence of computing and communications technologies are the Minitrends of virtual lives and interactive Web platforms. Within the Megatrend of long-term energy shortages are Minitrends of increased electrification of industrial processes and the development of advanced digital machines.

There are, of course, many Minitrends emerging that have little or no relationship with a Megatrend. These include trends such as the increasing participation in virtual worlds, the increasing number of people working at home, and the development of new approaches to the giving and receiving of advice based on information technology advances.

ROLE OF MINITRENDS

Megatrends normally fall under the aegis of governments and large international corporations; Minitrends, on the other hand, often have relevance to wider audiences. Although many Minitrends promise to grow increasingly important within the next few years, they are typically not recognized nor appreciated by the general public or most large companies. Employing the principles of Minitrend application can provide you with significant professional and personal advantages if you are alert enough to recognize emerging Minitrends, clever enough to realize their significance, and talented enough to take full advantage of the opportunities that they represent.

In today's business world, uncovering, analyzing, and acting on Minitrends can provide opportunities for individuals and small groups of individuals to establish successful new businesses, for small and medium-size businesses to expand and grow, and for large businesses to take advantage of significant changes in their operating environments. (In this book the term "individual" is used for a single person or for groups of six people or less; the term "large business" is reserved for companies that have revenues of at least $200 million per year or have 50,000 or more employees; and the term "small and medium-size companies" is used for companies between these two sizes.)

The purpose of this book is to assist you, the reader, in uncovering and analyzing promising Minitrends, to provide techniques for selecting specific Minitrends which merit follow up, and to present techniques for translating the identified Minitrends into profitable business opportunities. In the process of accomplishing these objectives, I make extensive use of the experiences of individuals, including myself, and organizations, including my own, that have been involved in the successful application of Minitrend analyses.

As mentioned in the preface, I use the term "gems" in the major section headings as a metaphor for Minitrends because both have inherent value, require effort to uncover, entail processing to achieve their full value, and, can be very valuable to their discoverer.

Minitrends and individuals

- In Dallas, Texas, in 1967, Rollin King and Herb Kelleher noted the growth in the size and number of businesses in the Texas cities of Dallas, Fort Worth, Houston, Austin, and San Antonio. They had the foresight to see that air traffic between these cities was destined to grow steadily over the coming decade and envisioned the business opportunities of an airline that provided dependable, economic, and friendly service, primarily to business customers. The result was the creation of Southwest Airlines.

  Currently, Southwest Airlines is the largest airline in the United States in terms of the number of passengers carried domestically. It maintains the world's second-largest passenger fleet of aircraft and in January 2009, reported its 36th consecutive year of profitability.

- In Austin, Texas, in 1984, Michael Dell, while still in college, noted the increase in the demand for personal computers. He observed that individuals were much more cost-sensitive about computers than businesses, and believed that he could eliminate many of the costs of buying computers by distributing them to customers by mail service. Mr. Dell dropped out of college to found

Dell Computer, Inc. The company focused on a "configure to order" approach to manufacturing, i.e., delivering individual PCs configured to customer specifications.

Starting with a capital of $1,000, the company grossed more than $73 million in its first year in business. In 1999, Dell overtook Compaq to become the largest seller of personal computers in the United States, and in February 2005, the company was listed in first place in *Fortune* magazine's ranking of the "Most Admired Companies." Current company net income is over $41 billion per year.

- In San Bruno, California, in February 2005, Steve Chen, Chad Hurley, and Jawed Karim, former PayPal employees, noted the increasing capacities of digital electronics, particularly in cameras and cell phones. They noted the growing ability of individuals to produce short film clips. They perceived a business opportunity in providing a method for individuals to distribute these film clips and for others to download these clips. Based on these factors, the three entrepreneurs founded **YouTube, LLC**. The company began operations in headquarters located above a pizzeria and a Japanese restaurant in San Mateo, California.

  YouTube reports that more than 65,000 new videos are being uploaded every day and that the site is receiving 100 million video views per day. In November 2006, the company was purchased by Google, Inc. for $65 billion.

- In the late 1990s, Romi Haan, a young Korean wife and mother, was frustrated by the time and effort required to keep the floors in her home clean and sanitary. Moreover, she noted that other Korean homemakers were similarly chagrined. To address these frustrations, Ms. Haan decided to develop a "steam mop." After several years of effort, she was able to bring to market a successful steam cleaner that uses high temperature steam to loosen and wipe away dirt, kill germs, mites, fungus and E. coli from any hard floor surface. To produce and market the new product, Ms. Haan established the **HAAN Corporation**.

In 2007 the HAAN Corporation had revenues of about $90 million and has now expanded into the United States.

- In early 2006, Tomoko Namba, a former McKinsey & Co. partner, noting the obsession of Japanese mobile-savvy youngsters with the latest electronic devices, launched the **DeNA Co, Ltd**. in Tokyo, Japan. The initial product of DeNA was "Mobage Town," a collection of online games, chat rooms and virtual characters, access-ible only by cell phone. The innovative feature of this product is that users were and still are able to use the programs free of charge. Users, however, are invited to take part in the site's social network service where they can buy, for real-world money, clothes, accessories, and even furniture and real estate for use in a virtual world.

  The new system was an immediate hit and by the end of 2007 had 11 million members and was logging more than 15 billion page-views per month. For the year ending in March 2008, the net profit at DeNA, reached 6.7 billion yen ($65.6 million), 80 percent of which comes from purchases on the site's social network. Re-cently, DeNA has opened up subsidiaries in China and the United States.

In many cases, flexibility, low overhead, and ability to move quickly provide individuals with unique opportunities to take advantage of emerging Minitrends. The principles and techniques presented in this book provide guidance for seizing such opportunities.

Minitrends and small and medium-size companies

Minitrend recognition is also of significant value to small and medium-size companies by alerting them to new business opportunities. In fact, the ability of smaller companies to suc-ceed in an environment in which larger companies have more resources, stronger financing, and greater staying power may well depend on keeping alert for emerging Minitrends and reacting rapidly to their emergence.

- **American Superconductor, Inc. (AMSC)** was established in 1987, shortly after the discovery of the high-temperature superconductivity (HTS) phenomenon. (HTS makes possible the transmission of electricity without current losses at relatively high temperatures.) Although a great deal of research and development was needed before superconducting wire could be produced in bulk quantities and utilized in practical applications, AMSC became the world's leading developer and manufacturer of HTS wire within a relatively short period of time. The company shortened the time from research to market by developing a variety of practical applications including power cables, motors, generators, and specialty magnets. But the story was not an immediate commercial success: despite a continuing series of product and process advances, the company failed to turn a profit for a number of years.

  In the early 2000s, AMSC noted an increasing demand throughout the world for clean energy sources, particularly wind energy. The transient nature of wind power, however, presents very serious technical problems, such as severe voltage fluctuations, excess stresses on gearboxes, and reduced equipment lifetimes. The management of AMSC saw the need for equipment to address these problems and, using the company's expertise in HTS, developed the superconducting D-VAR System to meet this requirement.

  The company's engagement in the wind energy arena represents an entirely new business line, and its wind power sector generated 65 percent of its sales in 2007. AMSC management is currently considering entry into the thermal solar energy area whose variable production characteristics are somewhat similar to those of wind power. AMSC is continuing to stay alert to attractive Minitrends.

- In many cases, important Minitrends may reflect changes in market demand. Companies must be alert to such changes and modify their strategies accordingly. For decades, watchmakers in Switzerland were acclaimed for the precision and accuracy of their products. A twenty-one jewel watch was the quality standard of the world. In the 1960s, however, electronic digital watches, which are extremely accurate, began to replace mechanical watches. Some of the more perceptive Swiss manufacturers recognized this trend and reacted by changing their concentration from the general timepiece market to a high-priced specialty market. Anyone could buy a Timex to tell the time, but only the sophisticated and well-to-do could show off a Rolex.

    In similar manner, U.S. bicycle manufacturers noted the public's increasing interest in health and environmental matters and converted their marketing effort (and products) from a low-cost means of transportation to a vehicle offering healthy and environmentally-friendly exercise. The fact that there are currently more than 2,000 bicycle manufactures throughout the world testifies to the success of this strategy.

- In a more personal area, my company, **Technology Futures, Inc. (TFI)**, represents an example of the importance of a small company taking advantage of emerging Minitrends. When TFI was founded in 1978, we concentrated on conducting research and training in technology forecasting in the petroleum industry. Our clients included most of the major companies in that industry, e.g., Exxon, Shell, Gulf, Continental, British Petroleum, Phillips, and Atlantic-Richfield. As time went on, we observed the increasing consolidation of these companies, while also noting increasing public interest in computers. Acting on the recognition of these trends, we increased our efforts in the computer area, and, at one time, the computer industry provided the majority of TFI's income.

During this period we also noted increasing interest in entrepreneurship, so we initiated a workshop and began consulting in this area. These efforts resulted in our being engaged by a number of companies and government agencies to promote entrepreneurial activities in their organizations.

In the mid-1980s, we took note of trends developing in the telecommunications industry, particularly in mobile communications, and began a concentration in this area. We assisted in the establishment of the Telecommunications Technology Forecasting Group, which is comprised of representatives from the nation's leading local exchange carriers. Currently, telecommunications consulting, research, and education provide more than half of our total revenue.

After the Twin Towers attack in 2001, we judged that there would be increased interest in national intelligence processes, so we initiated projects in that area. These projects became an important source of income for TFI as we conducted forecasts for the Central Intelligence Agency, the National Security Agency, and the National Geospatial Intelligence Agency.

Over the last couple of years we have noted increasing interest in the energy/environmental area, and we are in the process of enhancing our capabilities in this arena. Recently, we have conducted forecasts in areas such as the electrification production processes, fuel cells, hybrid electric cars, and home technology integration.

Overall, I am convinced that an ability to identify and react to emerging Minitrends has been essential to our company's survival and success for more than three decades.

Minitrends and large companies

The invested capital, trained labor forces, and established markets often motivate large companies to ignore or dismiss Minitrends. Normally, the difficulty and expense of making significant changes to established products, processes, and procedures discourages large companies from making such changes. Successful large companies, of course, do pay attention to trends, but normally they concentrate on larger trends because of the cost, time, and effort required for changes in strategy. Even large companies, however, should keep a radar on for Minitrends that may offer promising new business opportunities or threaten current business operations.

When large companies (or usually individuals or component groups inside the companies) note emerging Minitrends they believe have the potential of being a significant opportunity or threat, they most often act to acquire or partner with a company that has already established a position in that arena.

- **Demand Media,** a company headquartered in Santa Monica, California, specializes in distributing website content to existing large company websites and in creating website content for search engine queries. Recently, the company noted the increasing interest in RSS (Really Simple Syndication) feeds, a format for delivering regularly changing Web content.

  Demand Media became aware of Pluck, Inc., a leading on-line producer, publisher, and syndicator of professional content and social media solutions. Pluck utilized proprietary software to help mainstream media outlets syndicate blogs. These services coordinated well with Demand Media's own services, and, in March 2008, the company purchased Pluck to take advantage of its contacts and capabilities.

  Demand Media currently operates the world's largest blog syndication network that connects newspapers and other media sites to selected blogs. The company's software runs on more than 200 websites, including those of USA Today, The Washington Post, and Fox News.

  Demand Media recognized the emerging RSS Minitrend and the purchase of Pluck provided Demand Media with an opportunity to cash in on this trend.

- **Xerox Corporation** is one of the largest global document management companies in the world. It manufactures and sells a range of color and black-and-white printers, multifunction systems, photocopiers, digital production printing presses, and related consulting services and supplies. Although the company has been successful for more than a century, it is continually on the alert for developing trends that could affect its operations.

  In the late 1970s, Xerox became aware of Kurzweil Computer Products, Inc. (KCP), a company that had introduced the first system for recognizing omni-font optical characters in 1974. This computer program was capable of recognizing text written in any normal font, and a commercial version was introduced in 1978. LexisNexis adopted the program to upload legal and news documents from paper onto its nascent online databases.

  In 1980, Xerox bought KCP because of its interest in further commercializing paper-to-computer text conversion. Since then Xerox has continued upgrading the Optical Character Recognition device, now called Xerox TextBridge, and it continues to be a market leader.

- In January 1982, **AT&T**, acting under an agreement with the U.S. Department of Justice, divested itself of its seven Regional Bell Operating Companies or "Baby Bells." The managements of these local exchange carriers (LECs) realized that changes were in the air and supported the formation of the Telecommunications Technology Forecasting Group (TTFG) to examine emerging trends. TTFG contracted with Technology Futures, Inc. to assist in these examinations. Among the trends identified and analyzed were:

  - Adoption of local digital switching

  - Expansion of cell phone usage

  - Use of access lines on fiber digital loop carrier

- Growing market for digital communication services
- Expanding variety of imaging on Internet
- Significantly increasing utilization of household broadband services

Although the LECs reacted to these trends differently, these analyses provided and continue to provide, insights that are useful to the companies in strategic planning, investment decisions, and analyzing tax and depreciation allocation.

The cooperation of the TTFG members illustrates that Minitrends can sometimes assist groups of companies, as well as individual companies. Also note that each of the listed trends represents a combination of Minitrends. The expansion of cell phone usage, for example, is driven by a number of technical advances, changes in social norms, and different business models.

FAILURE TO RECOGNIZE MINITRENDS

Recognition of and action on emerging Minitrends can provide attractive opportunities to individuals and companies. Failure to recognize and appreciate emerging Minitrends, however, can result in serious problems for existing companies.

When they have been successful for a long period of time, both individuals and organizations are often prone to "stick to their own knitting," i.e., continue activities that had proven successful in the past. In many cases this mentality can lead to decline and disaster. Fewer than 30 percent of the companies listed on the Fortune 100 twenty-five years ago are still on the list today.

Often the primary reason for the demise of such companies has been a failure to recognize and react to changing trends. Individuals and companies are not done in by the bullets from the front, but the unrecognized bullets coming from the side or back. In today's world of increasingly rapid change, failure to keep abreast of developing trends is often a prescription for surprise and tribulation.

Examples of such failures include:

- The **Sharper Image Corporation** was founded in 1977 as a catalog business selling jogging watches. The company established retail outlets in 184 locations throughout the United States over the next twenty years, mostly in shopping malls. The company specialized in high-end electronics and special-interest gifts and featured open sales displays where potential customers could easily browse and closely inspect the products. In time, its retail stores accounted for 60 percent of the company's total revenue.

  Sharper Image showed agility in reacting to trends by shifting its emphasis from catalog sales to retail stores and, later, by utilizing eBay sales. The company grew and grew. Sharper Image remained alert to emerging trends in both its product lines and sales processes, and as a result its business remained successful for more than three decades. At one time, Sharper Image employed 2,500 people nationwide.

  The company, however, failed to appreciate the public's decreasing interest in high priced luxury items, the aggressive pricing policies of big box competitors like Best Buy, and the general decreases in large mall shopping. In February 2008, the company filed for Chapter 11 bankruptcy, blaming low sales, aggravated by a decline in consumer spending. Sharper Image failed to see the Minitrend "bullets" coming from unexpected quarters.

- **Wonder Bread** was introduced to the public in May 1921 by the Taggart Baking Company of Indianapolis, Illinois. The company was famous for being an industry pioneer. The original appeal of Wonder Bread was that it stayed fresh much longer than other breads. In the 1930s the Taggart Baking Company was one of the first bakeries to market sliced bread. In the 1940s the company introduced "enriched bread," adding vitamins and minerals to its loaves, and its bright red, yellow, and blue packages began appearing throughout the United States.

Although the Wonder Bread brand had a long history of innovation, its owners failed to appreciate the increasing preference of the younger generation, particularly in Southern California, for healthier whole-grain breads and "premium" loaves. Because of declining sales in that area, in August 2007, the current owner, Interstate Bakeries, Inc., announced that it would end production of Wonder Bread in the Southern California market, leading to a loss of 1,300 jobs.

- In Seattle, Washington, in 1971, Howard Schultz, the owner of a local coffee roasting and distribution company, noted the increasing affluence of the American public and their desire to receive gracious treatment in their daily activities. Schultz recognized that there was a market for small businesses featuring top quality coffee and an opportunity to relax in an attractive environment. To take advantage of these emerging Minitrends, Mr. Schultz initiated the very successful **Starbucks** chain which offers top quality coffee drinks in a friendly and relaxed atmosphere

Starbucks has a long record of appreciating Minitrends, but failed to recognize the trend that more economically-stressed customers were beginning to opt for similar, lower-cost drinks offered by fast food restaurants such as McDonald's. While still popular, in summer 2008, the Starbucks company announced the termination of 1,000 employees, and in November 2008, the company reported a 98 percent decline in profit for the third quarter of the year. To be more economically competitive, Starbucks has recently introduced a line of instant coffee.

Note that in each of these three cases, the company's success was based on its recognizing and taking advantage of emerging trends, while their later difficulties can be attributed to failing to identify and react to other emerging trends. The difficulties of General Motors, Bear Sterns, Circuit City, Mervyns, and Linens n' Things also serve as examples of what happens when companies fail to be alert to developing Minitrends. The lesson is individuals and companies must be constantly alert to emerging Minitrends in technologies, social norms, market demands, laws and regulations, and economic and financial realities for continuing success.

ALL VERY INTERESTING, BUT FRANKLY, SO WHAT?

Most start-up enterprises begin with major disadvantages in their competition with larger established companies. Established companies have successful products and loyal customers; they have proven supply, manufacturing, and distribution systems; and they enjoy financial superiority and powerful allies. Four out of five start-up companies fail within the first five years. A major reason that some start-up enterprises survive and, indeed prosper, is their ability to recognize and take advantage of Minitrends.

Ms. Haan and her steam mop, Dell's mail-order PCs, and Demand Media's smart acquisitions all brought in consistent smart profits, and will continue to do so, so long as the now established companies keep their radar open to Minitrends coming from all sides.

For small and medium-size companies, the Minitrends that are most valuable are those that can build on their current areas of business. Companies must be alert to developments in their own business areas and in related areas.

For large companies, emerging Minitrends may offer attractive opportunities for advancing, or protecting, their current product lines or for expansion into new business arenas. Because of the structure of large companies, an individual or a special group in the company is more likely to initially recognize an important Minitrend. Bringing the Minitrend to the attention of company management to determine how it might fit into the company's plans and strategies is then the responsibility of that individual or group.

In all of these cases, if you are to effectively take advantage of Minitrends, you must recognize and act on the trends at the appropriate time in their development: early enough in the development process that few others have recognized the trend's importance, but far enough into the development process that the trend is likely to continue, and that the financial payoff can be realized in a reasonably short period of time (two to five years).

◌ ◌

I hope the examples described in this chapter convince you of the potential value of recognizing and appreciating the importance of emerging Minitrends and of acting on this recognition and appreciation. The rest of this book is dedicated to demonstrating how you can use Minitrends to your own advantage and that of your organization. I begin this task in Chapter Two, where I present techniques that will assist you in identifying promising Minitrends.

Note that this book discusses the exploitation of Minitrends in a step-by-step manner. In reality, however, application of the process requires the adoption of a mindset that encompasses all of the elements of the concept.

II: Uncovering Minitrends

To find precious gems, seekers must be familiar with techniques for uncovering gems and have information about where such gems are most likely to be found. The same requirements are necessary for you to successfully uncover attractive Minitrends.

Chapter Two

Searching for Minitrends

In Chapter One, I describe how the ability to identify and evaluate promising Minitrends can provide significant advantages to those alert to their relevance and importance. This, of course, raises the question of how you can separate these key trends from the ever-expanding overload of information, analyses, and hype typical of today's environment. There are clear strategies that you can use to ferret out key developments from those that are irrelevant, transitory, or insignificant. In this chapter, I discuss some practical techniques for uncovering Minitrends, while, in Chapter Three, I provide sources of information, ideas, and insights to provide you with material for the application of these techniques.

Don't be overwhelmed by the number of techniques and sources listed in these two chapters. I realize that only the largest organizations or most dedicated individuals have the time and resources necessary to employ all of the listed techniques. The approaches and techniques of greatest value will depend on the individuals and organizations involved, their goals and objectives, and the resources available to them. I advise you to look over the material presented and only then decide which approaches and techniques are most appropriate for you. At that point you will be ready to develop a plan to employ them effectively.

In the following paragraphs I discuss Minitrend searching techniques that my colleagues and I find to be practical and effective.

FOLLOW THE MONEY

In the 1974 Watergate scandal, a secret source known as "Deep Throat" advised two reporters from the Washington Post that to solve the scandal they should "follow the money." Under the same principle, individuals seeking to discover and evaluate promising Minitrends, will do well to examine who will make money, who will lose money, and who will pay money if the trend is extended, curtailed, or modified. Careful analysis of these factors can provide very useful insights. The basic elements in such a search is to identify potential sources of funds—particularly new funds—and to determine what these sources are hoping to achieve with their funds. Listed below are several funding sources that can provide useful information in regard to interesting Minitrends.

Note: Although the search for Minitrends may uncover some opportunities for the funding of business activities, that is not the primary purpose for discussing the techniques in this section. The thrust of this section is to assist you in uncovering Minitrends. On the other hand, if this search also suggests possible sources of funding, so much the better.

Federal government

Government agencies, especially those of the federal government, have vast funds available for use on selected projects. Therefore, reasonable places to start searching for emerging Minitrends are federal budgets. In such a search, you should be particularly alert to areas in which new or increased funding is being allotted. You should also give attention to areas where there are decreases in funding, since these decreases can reflect changing policies or programs. Year-to-year changes in funding may reflect the emergence of a new Minitrend; however, increases or decreases in funding that continue for a number of years may provide a better picture of emerging trends.

The study of overall government budgets is a daunting task, so you will do well to concentrate on specific sources where the most important changes might manifest themselves. For example, the National Science Foundation (NSF) is specifically charged with supporting research on the frontiers of science and technology. The Foundation is required by law to report the projects that it supports and a review of supported projects can give valuable insights into the most advanced thinking in these areas. A Minitrend seeker with an established interest or business model in the sciences might start here.

Strategy: *Go to the NSF website, http://www.nsf.gov, select "Awards," then "Search Awards For."*

Another interesting approach for identifying forefront developments is to investigate the activities of the Small Business Innovation Research (SBIR) program. This program requires federal agencies with large extramural R&D budgets to set aside 2.5% of their annual research budgets for small companies to conduct innovative R&D projects.

Currently, eleven Federal agencies participate in the SBIR program:

- Department of Health and Human Services (DHHS)
- Department of Agriculture (USDA)
- Department of Commerce (DOC)
- Department of Defense (DOD)
- Department of Education (DOED)
- Department of Energy (DOE)
- Department of Homeland Security (DHS)
- Department of Transportation (DOT)
- Environmental Protection Agency (EPA)
- National Aeronautics and Space Administration (NASA)
- National Science Foundation (NSF)

Companies participating in the SBIR program may be awarded up to $100,000 over a six-month period to establish the technical merit and feasibility of their project and its potential for commercialization (Phase I). Companies may receive an additional $750,000 (Phase II) to continue the project if Phase I results justify it. Further government support may be authorized in Phase III to assist in commercialization, if warranted.

The Small Business Technology Transfer (STTR) program, established in 1992, is similar to the SBIR program, but applicants for this program are required to formally collaborate with a research institution in Phases I and II.

Currently the following organizations participate in the STTR program:

- Department of Defense (DOD)
- Department of Energy (DOE)
- Department of Health and Human Services (DHHS)
- National Institutes of Health (NIH)
- National Aeronautics and Space Administration (NASA)
- National Science Foundation (NSF)

The government agencies participating in either of these programs are required to announce the areas in which they are soliciting proposals and to identify the projects that they are funding. Thus, the agencies involved in these programs can provide a valuable screening task for Minitrend searchers by identifying those projects that have a high probability for commercial success.

Remember that at this point the purpose of examining these programs is not to identify potential funding sources as such, but rather to identify projects that are being proposed and/or funded in order to gleam attractive Minitrends.

Strategy: Each agency participating in the SBIR program and/or the STTR program has its own process for recovering information. For example, for information about the Department of Health and Human Services, go to its website, http://www.hhs.gov, and type in SBIR or STTR in the "Search" box.

In 1998, Technology Futures, Inc. (TFI) was contracted by the U.S. Central Intelligence Agency (CIA) to assist them in addressing a growing problem. The Agency was well aware of the necessity of keeping aware of developments on the forefronts of technology. Historically, the CIA had depended on the research and development laboratories of large companies such as IBM, Honeywell, and General Electric to provide such information. However, the Agency had begun to realize that the most truly innovative concepts were being developed increasingly by entrepreneurs, small growth companies, and university researchers.

Working directly with the government often placed restrictions on small companies' ability to capitalize on their intellectual property and on university researchers' publishing the results of their work. Naturally these groups were hesitant about partnering with the federal government and particularly hesitant about dealing with intelligence agencies because of security restrictions. Because of the secretive nature of its work, the CIA was being cut out of the most innovative technologies.

To overcome this problem, TFI, working with the Arthur Andersen Consulting firm and the Arnold and Porter LLP law firm, developed the concept that has grown into the very successful not-for-profit venture capital firm called In-Q-Tel. (The "In-Tel" comes from the term "Intelligence," while the "Q" acknowledges the super scientist associated with the James Bond series.)

The mission of In-Q-Tel is to identify and invest in cutting-edge technologies that can contribute to the security needs of the United States. The firm receives guidance from the government security agencies, e.g., the CIA, National Security Agency (NSA), and National Geospatial Intelligence Agency (NGA), on the types of technology in which they have interest. In-Q-Tel then determines the companies and researchers who are doing work in these areas and, where appropriate, provides funding. This approach allows entrepreneurs to develop their businesses as they see fit and allows university researchers to publish the results of their work.

Strategy: Since the projects supported by In-Q-Tel are, by definition, "emerging" and have been screened by In-Q-Tel for potential importance, a review of these projects can provide a powerful approach for recognizing interesting Minitrends. To conduct such a review, go to the In-Q-Tel website, http://www.iqt.org, and select "Technology Portfolio." Under this section, all of the projects currently sponsored by In-Q-Tel (currently about 80) are listed and a brief description of the technologies being developed by each company can be opened by clicking on the company's name.

Commercial organizations

Commercial organizations control a tremendous amount of capital. Review of annual reports, public announcements, and advertisements can reveal a great deal of information about their current activities and plans for the future. Many companies, however, are reluctant to disclose proprietary information. Even with the challenge of reluctant disclosure, people searching for Minitrends can be easily overwhelmed by the amount of information available. One approach for addressing these difficulties is to give special attention to the announcements of new business activities by major companies.

For example, in May 2005 General Electric announced a new program, "Ecomagination." This program was intended to "develop tomorrow's solutions" in areas such as solar energy, hybrid locomotives, fuel cells, lower-emission aircraft engines, lighter and stronger durable materials, efficient lighting, and water purification technology. The company indicated that it would invest $1.4 billion in clean-tech research and development in 2008 as part of this initiative.

In a similar fashion, in early 2008, JCI-SAFT Advanced Power Systems, a joint venture of Johnson Controls and Saft Groupe, SA, announced that it would begin production of lithium-ion battery packs at its plant in France for use in Mercedes-Benz and BMW hybrid vehicles. Analyses of large companies such as these undertaking new ventures may well suggest emerging Minitrends.

Strategy: Each year, Fortune magazine lists the 500 largest companies in the world on its website, http://money.cnn.com/ magazines/fortune/fortune500. The companies are organized in many different categories, e.g., relative size, industry, geographical location, and chief executive officer. The companies are also organized on various criteria, such as high revenue growth, high revenue to investors, and best companies to work for. Key information for each listed company can be obtained from this list, including a website address and a brief description of the mission and strategy of the company. A review of these descriptions can suggest those companies that might be looking for emerging business opportunities in your area of interest. When such companies have been identified, you can then go to the individual company's website to search for announcements of newly planned products or services. Often, these companies make it easy for you to sign up to receive annual reports, email updates, RSS feeds, blog posts, and Twitter tweets. (Visit http://minitrends.com/blog/what-is-rss for more on RSS feeds.)

Non-profit organizations

Under provisions of the United States Internal Revenue Code, certain non-profit organizations can be accorded exemption from federal income taxes. There are hundreds of such non-profit organizations dedicated to public benefits such as relief for the poor, advancement of religion or education, or defense of human and civil rights. Many of these organizations are well-funded and provide a great deal of money for selected programs. The goals and activities of these organizations are generally well-recognized and, normally, examination of their activities is not a very useful method for identifying new emerging Minitrends. However, the establishment of new organizations can be quite revealing of developing trends. To qualify for a tax exemption, an organization must make a formal application to the IRS—and these applications are open for public inspection.

Strategy: Go to the Wikipedia website, http://en.wikipedia.org/wiki/Category:Non-profit_organizations, which lists non-profit organizations by type and country. For example, selecting "Charities" and, then, "Educational Charities" will give you a list of such non-profit organizations. One of these organizations is "National Literacy Trust," and projects planned for the group are discussed in enough detail to determine if an important Minitrend is developing.

A foundation is a particular type of non-profit organization that may either donate funds and support to other organizations or provide the sole source of funding for their own charitable activities. Many philanthropic and charitable organizations are chartered as foundations. Although the nature of foundations varies between countries, in the United States, the Internal Revenue Code distinguishes between private foundations (usually funded by an individual, family, or corporation) and public charities (community associations that raise money from the general public). Private foundations have more restrictions and fewer tax benefits than public charities. Each of these has its own goals, operating procedures, and sources of funding.

Examples of private foundations include the Bill and Melinda Gates Foundation, established in 1999 and recognized as the world's largest private foundation dedicated to discovering new vaccines, educating more children, and bringing basic financial services to the poor around the world; the Alfred P. Sloan Foundation, established in 1934 to support original research and education in science, technology, engineering, mathematics, and economic performance; and the Pew Charitable Trusts founded in 1948, which applies rigorous, analytical approaches to improve public policy, inform the public, and stimulate civic life.

The activities of most foundations are well publicized and a review of their activities—especially new programs—can be very valuable for Minitrend searchers.

Strategy: There are a number of references under the term "Foundations" on the Google website, http://www.google.com, One example at http://www.foundations.org/grantmakers.html has about sixty listed alphabetically. You can click a foundation to find information about its organization, purpose, and activity. For example, if you click on the "Bill and Melinda Gates Foundation," you will be transferred to the foundation's website. Then selecting "Grants," will bring up a listing of all grants awarded by the foundation over the last year. Moreover, if you select "Email & RSS" at the bottom of the page, you can sign up for updates on future activities.

Venture capital firms

Venture capitalists often provide support for new approaches in both technical and non-technical areas. Although venture capitalists sometimes are reluctant to reveal their investments, there are a number of situations in which new companies make their plans available to potential investors. For example, Rice University conducts annual forums involving venture capitalists and companies with new products. Areas covered recently include nanotechnology, biotechnology, information technology, and energy and environment technologies. Examination of investments of venture capitalists often provides insights into leading edge developments.

Strategy: *There are a number of companies that list and describe venture capital firms. One of these is vFinance, Inc., http://www. vfinance.com, which lists more than 1400 venture capital firms and provides information on the size, preferred areas of investment, and contact procedures. The National Venture Capital Association website, http://www.nvca.org, also provides a list of venture capital organizations. Go to the website and select "Resources."*

FOLLOW THE LEADERS

Examine the comments and actions of people who have non-traditional visions—new approaches to solving world hunger, new applications of advances in technology, new social or political constructs. These are the individuals and their organizations that have the ability, resources, and contacts to make these visions realities. Although there are many factors that determine how trends and events develop, usually individuals are the drivers of how the future plays itself out. To utilize this approach, searchers must (1) identify those individuals who tend to be thought and action leaders, (2) examine the intentions and objectives of these individuals, and (3) determine the Minitrends that may be associated with the ideas and actions of these individuals.

Influential people

There are a number of publications that feature current leaders, as well as those just beginning to exert influence. Each year *Time* magazine publishes a list of the 100 most influential people in the world, together with brief descriptions of their visions and goals. To find the current list, go to the Time website, http://www.time.com, and select "Specials," then "Time 100." (Because the descriptions of these people are typically written by friends and associates, they tend to be very positive, so read these lists with a critical eye.)

The 2010 *Time* magazine list of the 100 Most Important People in the World includes:

- **Dr. Douglas Schwartzentruber**, Goshen Health Center, and Dr. Larry Kwak, MD Anderson Cancer Center, who are working on vaccines to reduce the risk of cancer.

- **Nate Silver,** Owner, FiveThirtyEight, who correctly predicted the winner of 49 of the 50 states in the 2008 presidential race, as well as all of the U.S. Senate races. Recently, FiveThirtyEight has expanded its political analyses to international races including those in Iran and the United Kingdom.

- **Zaha Hadid,** Owner, Zaha Hadid Architects, who, for more than three decades, has been involved in an uncompromising commitment to modernism, testing the boundaries of architectural design. Her work includes modern buildings throughout the world.

Fortune magazine publishes a list each year of the 50 most powerful women in the world, http://money.cnn.com/magazines/fortune/mostpowerfulwomen. The 2010 list includes:

- **Indra Nooyi**, Chairman and CEO, PepsiCo, who is pushing healthier products like orange juice with omega-3 fatty acids.

- **Angela Braly**, President and CEO, Wellpoint, who is seeking to maintain the U.S. health-care system's choice, flexibility, and cutting-edge treatments by encouraging consumer participation.

- **Ellen Kullman**, CEO, DuPont, who is seeking to work together with the company's customers on market-driven research and technical innovations. In the past five years, DuPont has established three R&D facilities in China.

In addition to these magazines, there are a number of groups that publish lists of important people in particular fields. These include among others:

- **The 50 Most Important People on the Web**, *PCWorld*,
  http://www.pcworld.com/article/129301/the_50_most_
  important_people_on_the_web.html

- **50 Who Matter Now**, by *CNN Money*, http://money.
  cnn.com/magazines/business2/peoplewhomatter

- **The 100 Most Influential People in Tech**, by T3,
  http://tech100.t3.com/list/100-81

Strategy: The people on these and other similar lists represent a group of influential individuals who play critical roles in all phases of our lives. Examining the interests and goals of people on such lists often provides useful indications of key future developments, including important Minitrends. The large number of people on these lists makes it all but impossible to monitor even a small fraction of them. A reasonable strategy is to scan the lists to identify and concentrate on those who have interests similar to your own.

> A different approach to looking at the influence of people on trends is offered in the book, *The101 Most Influential People Who Never Lived.* This book discusses how mythical personages such as Siegfried, Uncle Tom, Rosie the Riveter, Barbie, and Santa Claus have helped shape our culture and our lives. A review of the impacts made by these fictitious characters may suggest Minitrends that could develop from modern mythical icons, such as Luke Skywalker, Buffy the Vampire Slayer, and Harry Potter.

Movers and shakers

There are, of course, many well recognized people whose judgment is particularly valued and whose actions may portend significant Minitrends. For instance, when Warren Buffett announced that his Berkshire Hathaway company was investing three billion dollars in the General Electric Company, whose stock had decreased by more than 50% in the last year, and five billion in Goldman Sachs, whose stock had lost almost two-thirds of its value in the same year, one could not help but wonder what developments he foresaw in the business areas in which these companies operated.

Likewise when T. Boone Pickens, the well-known oil executive, announced that he planned to spend twelve billion dollars to build the world's largest wind farm (an investment that he later postponed when oil and gas prices declined sharply), it raised the question as to what truly drove both of these decisions.

Strategy: The names, associations, and activities of personalities like Mr. Buffett and Mr. Pickens are presented regularly in newspapers, magazines, television, and other media outlets. Statements or actions by these people that appear unexpected, unusual, or out of character can offer clues to the pending emergence of a new Minitrend. "Movers and shakers" come from a number of different fields—business leaders, government officials, political office holders and candidates, and media personalities. Movers and shakers are, by definition, people who "make things happen" and attention to current events will usually tell you who they are and what they are involved in.

Futurists

Examining the thoughts of individuals with special records of projecting future trends and events can also be useful in uncovering Minitrends. For example, **Raymond Kurzweil** has been a pioneer in the fields of optical character recognition (OCR), text-to-speech synthesis, speech recognition technology, and electronic keyboard instruments. He is the author of several books on health, artificial intelligence, transhumanism, and futurism.

Kurzweil gained a large amount of credibility as a futurist with the publication of his first book, *The Age of Intelligent Machines*. In this book Kurzweil forecast with considerable temporal accuracy:

- The demise of the Soviet Union due to new technologies, such as cellular phones and fax machines, that diminished authoritarian government's control over the flow of information

- The defeat of the best human chess players by a computer

- The explosive growth in worldwide Internet use and content

- The inevitability of wireless systems becoming the preferred mode of Internet access

- The existence of many documents existing solely on computers and the Internet

- The increasing reliance of the world's foremost militaries on more intelligent, computerized weapons, rather than large, low-tech armies

In 1999, Kurzweil published a second book titled *The Age of Spiritual Machines* that goes into more depth explaining his futurist ideas. In this book Kurzweil projects the status of technology in the Years 2009, 2019, 2029, and 2099. Of course, the accuracy of all but the first of these forecasts has yet to be demonstrated, and even he now admits that many of his projections for 2009 have not yet come to pass.

There are many other renowned futurists. A list of many such individuals, together with their fields of interest and most important works, is provided on the Wikipedia website, http://en.wikipedia.org/wiki/List_of_futurologists. The people on this list represent a wide range of interests, including business, technology, economics, society, and politics, among a host of others disciplines

The list does not, of course, include all of the capable and interesting futurists. Through the years I have had the pleasure of working with a number of outstanding futurists. These include, but are not limited to:

- **David Pearce Snyder**, president of Snyder Family Enterprises. David was one of the founding fathers of The Futurist magazine and for twenty years served as its Life Style Editor. He is well-respected in the business and government arenas as a speaker and consultant on issues involving future developments and trends. During his more than three decades in the futures business, David has compiled a multi-million item database which he uses to develop detailed future scenarios involving the most probable combinations of economic, technological, and social realities. Contact David at david_snyder@verizon.net.

- **Joseph Coates**, head of Consulting Futurist, Inc. has a long career as a futurist at the Institute for Defense Analyses, the National Science Foundation, and the Congressional Office of Technology Assessment. He has consulted for many Fortune 100 companies, numerous smaller firms, trade, professional, public interest, and foreign groups, and all levels of government. Joe has almost three hundred futures-associated articles listed on his company's Web page, http://josephcoates.com/articles.html. You may reach Joe by email at Joe@josephcoates.com.

- **Peter Bishop**, coordinator of the graduate program in futures studies at the University of Houston. Peter is active in a wide range of futures-related activities, specializing in techniques for long-term forecasting and planning. He was also a founding board member of the Association of Professional Futurists. Contact Peter at pbishop@uh.edu.

- **David Smith**, CEO of HBMG, Inc. David is a particularly perceptive individual who has held responsible positions in a number of business, academic, and research organizations, including Technology Futures, Inc. He is particularly interested and experienced in developing and utilizing Roadmaps, a strategic planning tool. Contact David at dsmith@hbmginc.com.

- **Oliver Markley**, principal of Inward Bound Visioning, a professional practice using the resources of higher consciousness for focused visioning, guidance, and transformation. Oliver is currently developing a suite of audible software programs for Imaginal Visioning and sustainable well-being. Contact Oliver at oliver@owmarkley.org.

- **Lawrence Vanston**, president of Technology Futures, Inc. (TFI). For two decades Larry has been involved in forecasting and analysis projects in the telecommunications area. He assisted in the establishment of the Telecommunications Technology Forecasting Group (TTFG) and was one of the first to appreciate the potential importance of wireless communications, online video, electronic imaging, and broadband to the home. Several of Larry's papers and reports are available at http://www.tfi.com. (I may be a bit prejudiced in the matter since Larry is my son.) Email: lvanston@tfi.com.

Strategy: The various futurist sources that I reference in this section will provide the names and associations of a large number of individuals who could prove useful sources of Minitrends. Checking with Google at http://www.google.com, Wikipedia at http://www.wikipedia.com, or Bing at http://www.bing.com, will give you information on their backgrounds and interests. When you find similar interests with one or more of these people, I suggest that you contact them, preferably by email, for more information about their activities and views. My experience has been that these people are very gracious (within reason) about sharing information and ideas.

EXAMINE LIMITS

In today's world, everyone's personal and business lives are bounded by a variety of technical, legal, economic, regulatory, and social limits. Consider such items as the battery lives of computers and cell phones, the limit on a person's credit card debt, and the limit on automobile speed on various roads. Often such limits can be impacted by advances in technology, changes in public attitudes and business practices, or unexpected trends or events. Often changes in limits lead to significant new developments and opportunities. People looking for important new emerging Minitrends are well served by examining relevant limits, defining the reasons for these limits, and searching for possible means for overcoming them.

Limits can usefully be divided into three general categories—physical, perceptual, and practical. Physical limits are normally defined by nature and cannot be exceeded. Examples include items such as the speed of light in a vacuum, the temperature of absolute zero, and the Carnot efficiency of an engine. Perceptive limits are those that are generally accepted by the public without any indisputable evidence. Examples include beliefs that airplanes could not exceed the speed of sound, that moving pictures couldn't be sent through the air, or that humans couldn't run a mile in less than four minutes.

Practical limits are those in which advances are possible, but which do not justify the time, effort, or expense required to make them. For example, for many years increases in the speed of commercial aircraft offered competitive advantages to both airlines and airplane manufacturers. Development of supersonic aircraft proved to be technically possible, but a combination of restrictions on the use of such aircraft over land routes, the large cost of operating them, and their high fuel usage resulted in their being withdrawn from commercial service in 2003.

> TFI, for a time, accepted the general belief that the minimum size of a mobile-phone cell was about one mile. (A "cell" in this usage is the geographical area served by a single transmission tower. The smaller the cell size, the more circuits that can be used in a given area.) We later found that this limit had been postulated in an early academic paper on the subject and actually presented no real limit. This realization allowed us to make more realistic projections about the growth of cell phones. Current cell sizes may be as small as 200 meters. In this case we were able to benefit from the recognition of the decreasing cell size Minitrend.

In practice, most non-technical limits are either perceptive or practical and, thus, are the types that can be altered if circumstances, public opinion, or driving forces change. A useful approach for taking advantage of changing limits to identify emerging Minitrends is to (1) identify the factors governing current limits, (2) be alert to changes in these factors, and (3) examine how the changing factors could modify the accepted limits. For example, a common factor limiting the adoption of a product or service is the cost of providing it. Thus, a reduction of these costs can overcome a limit to adoption and result in a new Minitrend.

The point is that a generally accepted limit often can be overcome by technical advances that provide new capabilities, reductions in prices, or changes in perceptions of key limitations. Examining the accepted limits to determine the factors governing these limits and searching for developments, technical or non-technical, that can modify these factors, can often allow imaginative people to identify emerging Minitrends.

Although physical limits cannot be changed, there are compelling examples where using different technologies can result in change within generally accepted limits. Consider that for decades it was believed in the physics community that "superconductivity" (the ability to conduct electric current in a circuit without power loss) could only be achieved at very low temperatures, i.e., a few degrees above absolute zero.

Superconductivity was largely relegated to basic physics studies because of this firm belief. However, in 1986 Karl Müller and Johannes Bednorz were able to demonstrate superconductivity in copper oxide ceramic material at a temperature of 77 degrees above absolute zero. Such substances were normally considered to be nonconductors or insulators. Further research has raised this limit to about 170 degrees above absolute zero. This ability to achieve superconductivity at higher temperatures makes possible their use for practical applications, such as powerful electromagnets used in Magnetically Levitated Trains (Maglevs), Magnetic Resonance Imaging (MRI), Nuclear Magnetic Resonance (NMR) machines, particle accelerators, fusion reactors, power cables, magnetometers, and ultrasensitive electronic signal receivers.

The discovery of high-temperature superconductivity reflected an entirely new research approach that has resulted in new limits on superconducting materials. It is interesting to note that this phenomenon had been observed several times by graduate students in various university laboratories, but had been dismissed as experimental errors.

Strategy: *You can identify limit-related Minitrends using either of two approaches: (1) you can examine current limits and consider how these limits might be relaxed or (2) you can stay alert to changing factors and consider how they might relax certain current limits. In either case, you are more likely to uncover promising limit-related Minitrends in areas where you have special knowledge, experience, and interest. In these areas you will have a better understanding of what is restricting improvements and how those restrictions might be overcome.*

CONSIDER HUMAN NATURE

It is important to remember that the timing, nature, and implications of emerging Minitrends (and Megatrends for that matter) are determined by the beliefs, motivations, and actions of humans—and that, basically, most aspects of human nature are reasonably discernible and predictable. If one considers the characters in the plays of Shakespeare, in the poems of the Roman poet Ovid, in the Greek tragedies of Sophocles and Euripides, and even in the hieroglyphics of ancient Egypt, they can be recognized in our daily lives. Their actions were driven by the same motives as ours—ambition, love, pride, fear, anger, sympathy, and fun. These characteristics should not be ignored when searching for emerging Minitrends in any age. It should be noted that, although the people's motives remain the same, the way that they satisfy these motives changes over time.

- People still want to establish meaningful long-term relationships—but difficulties in achieving financial security and more permissive sexual attitudes are leading people to postpone marriage and starting families.

- People still want to improve the lives of their children and realize the importance of education in meeting this goal—but the increasing costs of a four year college education are leading many people to take advantage of two-year colleges, distant learning programs, or enrollment in foreign colleges. (Between 1982 and 2007, four-year college tuition and fees in the United States, adjusted for inflation, increased 439 percent.)

- People still want to be involved with groups of friends—but an increased ability to form friendships electronically is changing the nature of related group dynamics.

- People still want to have top quality medical care—but the increasing cost of such care in the United States is causing an increasing number of people to go to other countries to receive such care.

The tendency of individuals to satisfy basic desires in different manners often drives the emergence of Minitrends.

In 1983, I was at Motorola's Schulenburg, Illinois, headquarters when the company announced the first commercial portable cellular phone. This phone was about the size of a cigar box (for those readers who have never seen a cigar box, they are about the size of a medium-size cereal box), weighed about five pounds, and cost about $3,000. At that time, the opinion of most telecommunications experts was that the phones were too big, too expensive, and too limited in capability to ever serve more than a niche market.

Our consultants at TFI, however, believed that these experts failed to appreciate the public's hunger for mobility, and in 1986 we published our first forecast on cell phones. In this forecast, we predicted that the cost of 250 minutes of cell phone service would be reduced from $145 to $40 by 1997 and that wireless telephony would compete effectively with wireline service by the late 1990s.

At that time, these forecasts were met with considerable skepticism. In actuality, by the Year 1997, the cost of 250 minutes of service had been reduced to $30, and, by the Year 2000, there were more than 100 million cell phone subscribers in the United States alone. The demand of the public for mobility drove dramatic advances in the related technology.

Strategy: Human behavior is, of course, a complex subject area. Google lists more than six million items on "Frustration," more than thirty-five million on "Affection," and more than two hundred million on "Fear." Establishing any reasonable process for analyzing human nature is difficult. Being alert to indications of changing public attitudes as represented by polls, surveys, formations of action groups, and media attention is, however, possible. Consideration of the driving forces behind these changes can give important insights into developing Minitrends.

TAKE NOTE OF DEMOGRAPHICS

Many futurists assert that the only real drivers of the future are climate and demography. In the last several years, considerable attention has been paid to both of these factors. In the area of demography, issues of immigration, population shift, birth rate, and the aging of the population are all important issues that merit careful consideration when seeking out Minitrends.

Considering the differences in goals, expectations, and viewpoints between the various age cohorts is useful. The largest age cohort in the United States is the "Millenniums" (people who came of age around the turn of the millennium). This group, having grown up in a world of laptops, cell phones, and the Internet, are very technically savvy. They tend to be quite sophisticated and dedicated to doing things "their own way." They tend to be more liberal than the older cohorts in terms of race relations, immigration, and government involvement in business affairs. They also are more dedicated in their commitment to assistance to the poor and underprivileged. They tend to be quite open about their personal lives, with a willingness to lay out secrets to total strangers through postings on MySpace, Facebook, Twitter, and blogs.

On the other end of the spectrum, the number of citizens 65 and older is growing each year. These seniors, however, are no longer willing to retire to their rocking chairs and old folks' homes. They are healthier, better educated, and, generally, more financially secure than people of their ages have been in the past. They are more interested in activities that can improve the quality of their lives, e.g., travel, entertainment, social interactions, and involvement in charitable activities. A recent study of 516 people between the ages of 70 and 104 by the University of Michigan and the Max Planck Institute for Human Development in Berlin found that older people today feel about 13 years younger than they actually are.

Between these two groups are what are generally referred to as Early Baby Boomers (born 1946–1955), Late Baby Boomers (born 1956-1965), and Generation Xers (born 1966-1976). The first of these groups came of age in a period of prosperity. They worked hard, spent lavishly, and expected to live a lifestyle markedly superior to that of their parents. Now that they are reaching retirement age, many are becoming concerned about their long-term financial security. The Late Boomers grew up in less prosperous times and tend to have a more realistic view of what life has to offer than the Early Boomers.

The Generation X cohort is probably the best-educated group in American history, with almost a third having bachelor degrees or higher. Sometimes referred to as the "Me Generation," members of this age group tend to be skeptical or even cynical about life. They tend to marry, form families, and commit to lifestyles later than other cohorts. The number of people in this cohort is considerably smaller than those before and after them.

Because of the disparate experiences of the different age cohorts and the resulting points of view, members of one age group may not understand or appreciate the opinions and actions of members of other groups. Many members of the older cohorts do not realize that the younger cohorts see the world in considerably different ways than they do. These older cohorts try to apply their experiences and value systems to the younger cohorts without realizing that, for the younger groups, these experiences and values are of little relevance. By the same token, the reverse is true.

These comments are, of course, generalizations and do not apply to all members of the various cohorts.

A few years ago, TFI was asked by a Canadian pharmaceutical company to assist them in developing a new business strategy using one of our planning tools, Technology Advantage Management. In using this tool, clients are asked to define what they believe the company should be doing in the future in terms of Nature of Change (Product, Process, or Procedure) and Degree of Change (Incremental, Distinctive, or Breakthrough). The clients are then asked to characterize the company's current programs in the same terms. The mismatches between "Should Be" and "Is" are then identified and plans made to alleviate the differences.

In this project we asked more than fifty employees in various departments at various management levels to rate the company in each category. The ratings were then averaged and the two results of Should Be and Is were compared. The two matrices matched almost exactly, which indicated that the company was apparently doing exactly what it should be doing. However, when we compared the answers by individuals, we made a surprising discovery. The ratings for younger employees who had been with the company for less than five years, were almost exactly opposite from those of older employees who had been in the company more than ten years. (Because of past hiring practices, very few employees had been with the company between five and ten years.) This fact indicated to us that the company had a major dichotomy between age cohorts, both as to what its current strategy was and what its future strategy should be.

Strategy: Each of the listed cohorts has its own way of looking at situations, strives for its own goals and objectives, and will react to events in its own way. Careful examination of differences and similarities in the perspectives of the different age cohorts can uncover useful Minitrends.

ANALYZE FRUSTRATIONS

Daily life presents people with many situations that they find troublesome, annoying, and disconcerting—long waits at restaurants, mosquitoes at picnics, surly salesclerks, etc. Such frustrations are shared by a large segment of the public. Sometimes consideration of these frustrations, together with possible means of alleviating them, can lead to the uncovering of Minitrends.

In 1997 Reed Hastings was dismayed to find that he was being charged $40 for the late return of the movie *Apollo 13* to a local distributor. Since this was about three times the cost of the videocassette, he was both startled and incensed. Later that day he went to visit his athletic club and, while there, he noted the business model of the club. People paid a monthly fee to belong to the club and were then entitled to use the club's facilities as much as they wished during that month. Since there was a limited amount of exercise equipment at the club, there were times when certain items were not available. When that occurred, the member would typically use a different piece of equipment or, in some cases, simply wait until the equipment became available.

After some thought, he decided that these principles could be applied to the rental of the new smaller, cheaper, CD-based digital movie format, the DVD, in order to eliminate the problems of late return fines. He realized that this was a frustration that he probably shared with many other renters. This germ of an idea was put into application in 1997 when Reed and his friend, Marc Randolph, launched the *Netflix* company. When using this service, customers pay a set fee for the freedom to have in their possession at any given time a certain number of DVD movies. (The number depends on the size of the subscription, i.e., the larger the fee, the greater number of DVDs the customer can have at one time.) Customers typically provide a list of titles that they desire to receive in order of preference. These requests are mailed to the customer in this order. If the first movie on the list is not available, the next one is sent instead.

Once a customer has received their DVDs, he or she can keep them as long as desired. Thus there are no late fees. However, in order to receive a new DVD, customers must return a movie that they currently have. This procedure has proven very attractive to many customers and more than a million DVDs are sent out every day to the company's eight and a half million customers. The company currently has more than 100,000 different titles on hand, drawn from the work of most of the major film and television producers, as well as many independent and foreign producers. In keeping with the company's relaxed and labor-friendly personnel policies, workers are allowed unlimited vacation time and can take any amount of their paychecks in stock options.

Interestingly, the founders of Netflix—always alert to emerging Minitrends—understand the threat of competition such as DVD kiosks in grocery stores and other public locations and are already addressing strategies to address this growing competition. For example, in 2007 they began allowing their subscribers to stream videos directly to their PCs from the company's website.

Strategy: A potential approach for uncovering emerging Minitrends is to identify frustrations that are being experienced by large groups of people and to consider ways in which these frustrations can be addressed. You should give particular attention to frustrations in your own personal life, your business activities, and your various associations. Since these frustrations are the ones with which you are most familiar, they are the ones to which you can bring special expertise.

SEARCH FOR CONVERGENCES

Scientists and engineers have long found that key breakthroughs often occur when one technical development interacts with another. The modern computer would not have been possible without the development of transistors and microcircuits; the space program would not have been practical without computers; and global positioning systems could not have been developed without space satellites. Practical techniques for mapping individuals' DNA are making individually-targeted treatment of diseases practical, and developments in material sciences have made novel new building processes and high performance equipment possible. Recent developments in fuel cells for laptops and other electronic equipment promise to support the development of fuel cell powered automobiles.

In addition to the convergence of technologies, overlaps of new technologies with non-technical trends, convergence of new technologies with emerging market needs, and convergence of different non-technology trends can also illuminate new possibilities for Minitrends. For example, recent research in the use of nanotechnology materials to remove arsenic and other contaminants from water promises to ease the shortage of water throughout the world. International trade agreements, together with improvements in transportation technologies, have made the availability of seasonal fruits and vegetables for Americans possible throughout the year. The development of low-cost, solar-driven laptops (currently $187 each with a goal of $100) under the "Laptop for Every Student" project will undoubtedly prove a significant boon to students all over the world.

Often, when meaningful convergence occurs, important Minitrends result.

A few years ago we at TFI were asked by large medical supply company to assist them in identifying an entirely new product. This was a particularly daunting challenge since there had not been a major new development in the area for almost five decades. After conducting a number of interviews with groups within the company and with customer groups, we were able to identify a potential product that would have definite customer appeal. However, there was general agreement in the company that developing the product was not feasible. Basically, there were three technical problems that would have to be solved before the product could be developed.

On investigation we found that each of these problems had actually been solved, but at separate laboratories within the company. When we noted the convergence between these technical solutions, development of the product (a new type of bandage) went forward, and the product turned out to be very successful.

Strategy: When you are seeking to identify emerging Minitrends, you should not only examine individual trends, but also consider potential interactions between these trends.

ALL VERY INTERESTING, BUT FRANKLY, SO WHAT?

In the previous sections of this chapter, I discuss a number of techniques for uncovering potentially useful Minitrends. Although each of these techniques has its own features, its own benefits, and its own shortcomings, most share an important characteristic—their effective application requires time, effort, and discipline. Because of this, I recommend that you choose one or, at most two, of these approaches on which to concentrate.

Involve yourself in an approach that you are confident that you will enjoy. There's no point in undertaking an endeavor that doesn't add pleasure to your life. If you are interested in politics and policies, you may want to concentrate on examining government programs described in the "Follow the Money" section. If you enjoy studying biographies, you may want to engage yourself in the "Follow the Leaders" approach. If you have an engineering or scientific bent, you may want to utilize the "Examine Limits" approach.

In any case, the conduct of the search should be an enjoyable endeavor. If the search contributes to your effectiveness in your job, coincides with a hobby, and/or can make your personal life more enjoyable and satisfying, so much the better!

Once you decide on the approach to use, drawing up a search plan is the next step. To develop this plan you need to:

- Determine how much time you can devote to the project and how and when this time will be spent.

- Identify the subject areas you are going to search.

- Outline how you are going to record the results of the search.

- Clearly define the goals of your search and how you are going to measure how well you have accomplished these goals.

- Define intermediate goals so you can periodically assess your progress.

- Consider the circumstances where abandoning the selected approach and moving on to another one makes sense.

Note that the information gathered and insights developed during these searches may also be very valuable in converting the identified Minitrends into successful business opportunities. (I discuss such conversions in Chapters Seven, Eight, and Nine.)

If none of the listed approaches appeal to you, you may decide to utilize the Reed Hastings (Netflix) or Tomoko Namba (DeNA) (remember her from Chapter One?) approach and simply wait for a useful Minitrend to manifest itself to you. This approach certainly requires less time and effort than a more formal approach. However, you may want to ask yourself how many times such earth-shaking "bolts from the blue," revelations have proven successful for you in the past.

In this chapter, I outline some strategies for searching for promising Minitrends. In the next chapter, I suggest some sources of information and insights that will allow you to apply these strategies more effectively.

Chapter Three

Where to Search
for Minitrends

In Chapter Two, I discuss techniques for uncovering Minitrends. In this chapter, I list some information sources to use in applying these techniques. You can utilize these sources as part of a dedicated effort to uncover Minitrends, or you can simply be alert to emerging trends as you use the sources for other purposes. In either case, having a plan on how to proceed with your search is useful.

UTILIZE PUBLISHED SOURCES

Although electronic data search services are increasingly powerful and easy to use, you can still uncover a great deal of useful information from printed sources such as newspapers, magazines, company publications, and books. The real problem is separating out useful information from the vast amount of printed material available. You can use the following approaches to meet this problem.

Use scanning techniques

With this approach, you quickly review material, taking care not to concentrate on any one item. You should record or highlight items that might be of real interest for more careful study later. This technique requires a considerable amount of discipline at first because there is always a strong incentive for you to stop and read items of particular interest to you as you go along.

Take advantage of editorial assists

A number of newspapers such as *The New York Times*, *The Washington Post*, and *The Wall Street Journal*, present short synopses of major stories in a special section on or near the front page of the paper. Likewise, many magazines such as *Time* and *Newsweek* emphasize the key points of their articles in specially marked outtakes. These items can provide you with useful scanning surrogates.

Taking advantage of knowledge of the publication's structure of articles can also improve the efficiency of your searches. For example, in most news stories, the key information is presented in the first one or two paragraphs. In contrast, *The Wall Street Journal* often starts articles with a human-interest story that adds color to the article, but typically provides little information of import until later in the article. Articles in the *Scientific American* magazine typically follow a three-part format: the first part targets the general audience with a reasonable technical background; the second part of the article goes into considerable technical detail and is primarily valuable to those quite knowledgeable in the subject area; and the last part typically discusses the importance of the material included in the first two parts.

Utilize a wide range of information sources

To pick up less widely recognized information, you should make a point of reviewing at least one new information source each week. Most people tend to concentrate their reading efforts on areas in which they are particularly interested. By forcing yourself to look at other information sources, you open yourself up to new ideas, insights, and information that will help you to uncover Minitrends you might otherwise overlook.

There are a number of guides to help you in identifying a variety of useful information sources. For example, *All You Can Read* lists the top magazines in each of 48 categories at http://www.allyoucanread.com/top-10-magazines. Log onto this site, select a category, and then a magazine to review. *The New York Job Source* lists the 100 magazines with the largest circulation, http://nyjobsource.com/magazines.html.

To search for books on a given subject, log onto the Amazon website, http://www.amazon.com, and select "Books" in the first search box. Then type the subject in which you are interested in the second box. The website displays a list of all books on that subject in their catalog. Amazon is also organized so that if you select a book on a given topic, it provides a list of similar books that might be of interest. Amazon often provides a brief preview of the book and sometimes a small extract from the book that will give you an understanding of what type of information the book contains.

An interesting device for making printed material available to Minitrend searchers is the "Kindle," introduced in the United States by Amazon, Inc. in November 2007. This device uses an electronic display of books, magazines, newspapers, and selected blogs and can store large numbers of printed items. One fun feature of Kindle is that users can also play music from MP3 files as background music while they are reading. Amazon currently has more than 630,000 titles available at very reasonable prices for wireless download. With continuing Kindle updates and the recent introduction of the Apple iPad and e-book pressures from Google and other booksellers, the importance of e-books as a Minitrends tool continues to grow.

Establish a method for storing and accessing useful ideas and information

Often readers find information or ideas whose value is not readily apparent, but which may become useful in the future. Therefore, you should establish a system for storing these bits of potentially useful information, as well as a system that allows you to easily find and recover the stored items. Dramatic increases in storage capacity of computers, voice recorders, personal digital assistants (PDAs), cell phones, and digital cameras over the last few years make the establishment of such systems much easier to develop and maintain than in the past.

Social bookmarking services such as Delicious, http://delicious.com/help/learn, can help by bookmarking Web pages online, as well as show you what others are bookmarking across many areas of interest.

UTILIZE ELECTRONIC RESOURCES

Although a vast amount of information is presented as printed material, electronic data sources are often an easier and quicker way to gather information to identify possible Minitrends. Most newspapers and many magazines offer their printed material online. For example, you can call up articles from *The New York Times* by logging onto their website at http://www.nytimes.com, from *The Wall Street Journal* at http://www.wsj.com, and from *The Washington Post* and *The Washington Times* at http://www.washingtonpost.com and http://www.washingtontimes.com, respectively. In a similar manner, you can find articles from *Scientific American* by logging into http://www.scientificamerican.com, *Time* magazine by logging onto http://www.time.com, and *The Economist* at http://www.economist.com.

Current search engines and software agents provide the capability to locate desired information efficiently. Calling up a subject on Google at http://www.google.com, Yahoo at http://www.yahoo.com, Bing at http://www.bing.com, Ask at http://www.ask.com, or similar search engines, typically brings up a vast number of related articles. For example, a Google of "Trends" lists 179 million references. Most search engines utilize complicated algorithms to organize the listed items so that they will be of most value to the users, i.e., the most valuable item will appear near the beginning of the listed items. Google, for instance, uses more than 200 different factors, including age, sex, location, and search history of people conducting searches to better rank the listed items. In addition, Google normally displays a list of possible sub-items to make searching easier. For example, under "Trends," the display will list "Trends 2009," "Trends International," and "Trends Magazine," among others.

Another way to start a search is to find a related Wikipedia article. These articles are typically presented in a language and style easily understood by a layperson. To access Wikipedia articles, log onto http://www.wikipedia.org and enter the subject and language in the appropriate boxes. For example, I recently entered the term "nanotechnology" on the site and was given a choice of articles involving history, implications, applications, regulations, organizations, and references in fiction and popular culture, as well as a listing of related Wikipedia areas. (Wikipedia reports that it has stored 10 million articles in 253 languages.)

I, personally, often use the Ask engine because I can present my query in a question form. For example, when I ask, "What are today's most important trends?" I get a listing of references about trends, including one titled, "The 30 Most Important IT Trends for 2009." Another site that I often use to either verify or disprove questionable information that I receive is *Snopes*, http://www.snopes.com. This site indicates whether a given bit of information is "True," "False," or "Undetermined" and explains why the rating is given.

Other websites I find valuable for gathering information on a variety of different subjects are Alltop, http://alltop.com, About.com, http://www.about.com, SmartBrief, http://corp. smartbrief. com/about, and StumbleUpon, http://www. stumble upon.com/ aboutus.

Reference to printed material on-line has been made much easier by a recent $125 million investment by Google, allowing the company to make many millions of copyrighted, out-of-print works available digitally on the Web. The company has already scanned more than seven million books for its Google Book Search program. Individuals and institutions can gain on-line access to the books through Google, and free on-line viewing at public libraries. Richard Sarnoff, chairman of the Association of American Publishers, states that the agreement breathes new life into millions of books.

ENGAGE KEY ASSOCIATIONS

The number of associations—from professional to hobbyists—is almost limitless, ranging from the Association of Bearded Santa Clauses to the Federation of American Scientists. Most of these associations have officers and offices, many have websites and periodic publications, and many conduct annual or semi-annual conventions and meetings, often in attractive locations. In the associations' publications and meetings many interesting ideas and concepts are presented.

However, because of the vast number of associations, keeping abreast of all of the information provided by these associations is impossible, and even identifying the associations that are most relevant to you or your organization provides a significant challenge.

Fortunately, there are tools to help. The American Society of Association Executives provides listings of various associations, their missions, their organizational structure, their activities, and contact information, http://www.asaecenter.org. This information can be useful in determining the associations that are most promising. Wikipedia also presents a list of professional organizations at http://en.wikipedia.org/wiki/List_of_professional_organizations.

Associations that are specifically organized for the analysis of emerging trends include:

- World Future Society, http://www.wfs.org
- Rand Corporation, http://www.rand.org
- Institute for the Future, http://www.iftf.org
- International Institute for Applied Systems Analysis, http://www.iiasa.ac.at
- Centre for European Policy Studies, http://www.ceps.be
- Economic and Social Research Institute, http://www.esri.ie
- Club of Rome, http://www.clubofrome.org
- National Institute for Research Advancement, http://www.nira.or.jp/english
- Association of Professional Futurists, http://www.profuturists.org
- Strategic Planning Society, http://www.sps.org.uk

Association conferences and conventions can be powerful sources of information on emerging developments. The information and ideas presented at these conventions are on the forefront of the area involved, and you can normally follow-up on issues brought up in the formal sessions in later conversations with speakers and participants. The people you meet at these conferences can prove to be very valuable contacts. Announcements for the conventions and conferences typically list the backgrounds and special interests of speakers.

You can use this information to determine which of these people are worth following up on and how to elicit their interest when you contact them.

Many conferences also have associated exhibits where sponsoring companies display their products and services. Since the companies are anxious to put their best feet forward at these exhibits, they will typically showcase their most advanced products. They also have very knowledgeable representatives, sometimes even high-level officials, at their displays to present information about their products and about the company itself. These representatives are almost always extremely polite and open to conversation.

At some conferences there are associated book signings. Participating in such signings can add materially to the value of attending the conference. Conference speakers may be discussing recently published books in the area of their presentation, and attendance at the author's book-signings allows you to engage in personal conversations that are impossible during formal presentations. (It is not absolutely necessary to buy the book involved—but it is probably a good idea.)

The cost of attending conventions and society meetings in terms of time, money, and effort is quite high. Being selective in deciding the ones in which you will participate is important. At some conventions, particularly those in big cities, you may be able to register to visit the exhibits and even attend one or more of the keynote addresses at no charge.

In many cases, proceedings of conferences and sometimes even videos of selected presentations are available on the conference or association's website. You may wish to review the proceedings if attending a key conference is not practical. In doing this, however, the techniques previously discussed for scanning should be employed, since there will often be a considerable amount of material that is not truly relevant to your purposes.

A few years ago, a large industrial chemical company asked Technology Futures, Inc. to assist them in revising their surveillance program. The company had a rather elaborate process for evaluating and recording information about competitors' activities gained from employees who attended industry conferences. However, the management noted that they were not receiving as much information from these sources as they thought they should. Our staff interviewed a number of these attendees to determine the reasons for this.

What we found was that many of the attendees were unsure of the professional ethics involved in this activity and thus hesitated to report proprietary information they gathered at conferences. The company was not interested in encouraging unethical behavior, but we advised that by clarifying what was considered ethical among various professional groups, the company would benefit.

We worked with the company in developing a seminar for such clarification and a committee was formed to explain what was considered proper conduct. This committee presented their findings to employees throughout the world, and we were pleased to hear later that the amount of information being reported had increased markedly.

At about the same time we conducted this project, The Wall Street Journal presented an article on accepted procedures in the computer business. It was noted, for example, that if a person entered a bar it would be considered inappropriate to select a place near two people from a competing company in hopes of overhearing proprietary information. On the other hand, if these people happened to sit near, listening to their conversations was acceptable—but not taking notes. Conversations overheard in a restroom, however, were always fair game.

ESTABLISH SOCIAL NETWORKS

The value of social networks

Although college students are counseled to "keep up with the literature," a recent study found that two-thirds of useful information came from discussions with colleagues and, of the third found in the literature, more than half were recommended by colleagues. Given this fact, it is obvious that the more people with whom you are involved, the more useful ideas you will receive. If you wish to uncover important Minitrends, establishing as wide a range of friends and acquaintances as practical is highly desirable.

As I discuss in the previous section, joining local business, professional, civic, charity, and social organizations can expand your circle of acquaintances. Attending public lectures, involving yourself in community activities, serving on professional committees, and attending college courses can provide personal contacts with numerous people who may expand your views and, perhaps, suggest useful Minitrends.

Although I find that actually meeting with other people is the most satisfying and profitable means for interacting with others, this requires a considerable commitment of time and effort. The emergence of Web-based social networking platforms, such as LinkedIn, Facebook, and MySpace makes it much easier to expand your acquaintance base than was previously possible. These platforms also make it much easier to maintain contact with that base. Although most of the social networking platforms are free and have similar structures, each has special features that determine its value to people seeking to identify promising Minitrends. In the box below I briefly discuss several of the most popular social networking platforms.

A Sampling of Social Networking Platforms

LinkedIn, http://www.linkedin.com, is a business-oriented site specifically designed to assist users in establishing and maintaining professional contacts with people they know and trust. Individuals and companies can invite anyone to join their contact network made up of direct connections, second degree connections (connections of direct connections), and third degree connections (connections of second degree connections). You can expand your circle of business (and personal) acquaintances by establishing relationships with the contacts of your own direct contacts. You can also establish new relationships by joining the alumni, industry, professional, or other relevant groups maintained by the platform. A popular feature called Answers lets you ask business-related questions of people who might know. For my purposes, I find this to be the most useful platform.

Facebook, http://www.facebook.com, is structured to support contacts between members of specific networks. Each member provides personal data about himself or herself and, if desired, a personal photo. These networks are sometimes organized by workplace or school to make targeting easier. Members of a network can send messages to all members of their group or to an individual member. This platform is primarily designed and used for social interaction rather than professional purposes. Facebook Fan Pages, however, are now becoming very popular with individuals and companies seeking a more open platform environment. These pages are normally open to anyone. Facebook recently announced hitting 500 million users worldwide.

MySpace, http://www.myspace.com, is another social networking platform with an interactive, user-submitted network. Although this platform is often compared to Facebook, MySpace allows more extensive use of music, graphics, images, and layouts. For example, MySpace permits users to "dress up" their homepage with graphic backgrounds and indicate their moods by the use of small emoticons. Although losing ground to Facebook across the board, MySpace tends to have a higher percentage of younger users than Facebook, perhaps because they prefer the more visually stimulating site.

Twitter, http://www.twitter.com, is a social networking service that enables users to send and receive short text-based posts (tweets). Because of the limitations of the Short Message Service (SMS), the communication service standard on which Twitter messaging is based, these tweets are limited to 140 characters. Tweets can be delivered to all members of an established network, called "followers," or restricted to a specific member of the network. Many individuals have become very influential through attracting huge numbers of followers. Public acceptance of Twitter—particularly for mobile communications—has been very rapid with the number of registered users now listed at over 100 million. Twitter is estimated to be the third largest social network in the world after MySpace and Facebook. However, a recent Nielson Rating Service study indicated that the percentage of a given month's users who come back the following month is currently only about 40%. Tools such as Seesmic, http://seesmic.com/products/web, and TweetDeck, http://www. tweetdeck.com/desktop, make the management of multiple Twitter contacts much easier.

Skype, http://www.skype.com, is probably the platform most conducive to Minitrend related communications since it involves both voice and video interactions. Members can link, free of charge, to other members throughout the world. They can engage in either peer-to-peer communications or in a group mode. Currently, there are more than 520 million Skype users. Originally, the network was known as Sky Peer-to-Peer which was to be shortened to Skyper. However, this URL was already in use so the founders solved the problem by dropping the final "r."

Plaxo, http://www.plaxo.com, is a platform that facilitates users' ability to maintain contacts with those individuals or organizations that they believe are important to them, e.g., friends, family, business associates, classmates, etc. Those users who are registered with the platform (currently more than 40 million) can obtain current contact information from the Plaxo database. Plaxo is now a subsidiary of Comcast and its Pulse platform allows Plaxo to operate, in some respects, like a social network in which information, opinions, and photographs can be exchanged.

MyFace, http://www.myface.com, is another primarily social network much like Facebook and MySpace. Users can, however, be a bit more open in their communications because they can remain anonymous if they wish. Members can participate in forums, rate movies, share pictures and videos, and create their own music lists.

Ryze, http://www.ryze.com, is designed to assist professionals in making connections and growing their businesses through personal contacts or through business networks. More than 1,000 organizations host networks on Ryze.

Xing, http://www.xing.com, is a global network designed to assist members in managing contacts. Its membership includes 9 million business professionals throughout the world. Communications are conducted in 16 European, Asian, and Middle Eastern languages.

Foursquare, http://foursquare.com, is a location-based social network that is increasing in popularity as cell phones with GPS are becoming more common.

Smaller, niche social networks can sometimes be effective for spotting usable Minitrends in your particular area of interest. Wikipedia offers a directory of some of these at http://en.wikipedia.org/wiki/List_of_social_networking_websites.

Social platforms can provide an almost unlimited number of contacts. However, because most of these platforms are designed primarily to promote social interactions, identifying those contacts that may lead to interesting Minitrends is a challenging task.

To some extent, this task is simplified by the fact that participants are usually identified by age, sex, locality, and special interests. The best approach is usually to simply jump in and test the water. As you gain experience with the structure and processes of a platform, you can more easily identify and engage the people with whom you wish to interact.

Managing social networks

The use of the social networks can open an almost unlimited number of information and insight sources. The strength of using these networks is, however, also a weakness. Unless you apply a personal discipline when utilizing this approach, you may be easily overwhelmed by the number of people with whom you may become involved.

The following steps allow you to take maximum advantage of social networking without it becoming a sinkhole for your time and effort.

Select the general subject area in which you wish to receive new information and insight

Keeping your eyes open for promising Minitrends in any area is in your interest. Practical limits of time and effort, however, will restrict those in which you can make detailed analyses. You should decide on a general area on which to concentrate your social networking efforts. This choice can be based on past experience, current employment or position, suggestions from friends or family, or areas of personal interest including hobbies and pastimes.

You should select an area broad enough to uncover a range of promising Minitrends, but narrow enough to prevent excessive diversion of effort. Examples of the types of areas that might be selected include "the role of virtual worlds in education," "recent changes in how advice is offered and received," and "changing roles for senior citizens in the work-place."

Identify the people who can give you the most valuable information and insights

As indicated in the description of social networking approaches, there are a number of platforms that can help you to identify and contact people with interests in the area on which you plan to concentrate. Utilization of search engines such as Google, http://www.google.com, or Wikipedia, http://www.wikipedia.com, can also provide useful starting points for this activity. For example, searching Google for "Virtual World Education" provided me with a listing of related conferences, recent papers, forefront technical developments, contacts, and a host of other useful information. In many cases, these items indicate the areas of special interest of subject matter experts and, often, information for contacting these people.

Another way to find subject-matter experts is to participate in "blogs," "wikis," and "Internet forums." Involvement in these activities also facilitates the transfer of ideas and information between you and others. Google Blog Search, http://www.blogsearch.google.com, Wikipedia's list of wikis, http://en.wikipedia.org/wiki/List_of_wikis, and Big Boards' list of forums, http://directory.big-boards.com, can help in your search. The websites mentioned on page 51 can also be useful.

A **blog** (Web log) is a type of website established by an individual or organization in which opinions, comments, information, descriptions of events, and, in some cases, pictures, videos, and music are posted on a regular basis. Blogs often focus on a particular area of interest, e.g., politics, travel, technologies, and business activities. The blog manager or sometimes guest bloggers post an initial entry and other people can respond with comments on the post. Since people tend to participate regularly on specific blogs, you can develop insights on the interests, expertise, and viewpoints of not only the primary blogger, but also other participants. By participating, you may develop continuing relationships with the blog participants. Free services like Google Reader, http://www.google.com/intl/en/google reader/tour.html, help manage blog activity.

A **wiki** is a type of website used to develop collaborative databases in an area of interest to its creator and/or manager. (The name is based on the Hawaiian word for "quick.") Wikis can be used for many purposes such as intranets, knowledge management, and the sharing of information and ideas. A wiki encourages users to edit documents created by other users or to initiate their own wiki. In most cases, any input from users, such as document corrections, are accepted by the wiki. The theory is that other users will correct inaccurate or malicious input. Since the development of a wiki is an ongoing process, your participation can provide contacts with other people with similar ideas and interests. Wikipedia is an example of a large-scale wiki.

An **Internet forum** is an online discussion site organized to promote discussions among groups with common interests. These forums typically have participation rules which are established and monitored by their creators. To participate, you must apply and be accepted into the forum. The main subjects for discussion are called "threads" and contributions are called "posts." Typically, members can make unlimited posts to the forum. Some nations such as Japan and China have very large national forums. (Japan's largest forum has more than two million posts per day.) In the U.S. most of the several hundred Internet forums are relatively small and often narrowly focused.

Engage these people to provide information and insight

When you identify the people who you believe can provide you with useful information and insight, the next question is how to convince them to engage with you. Not surprisingly, the people with the most valuable insights and information are often those with the busiest schedules and greatest time constraints. I find, however, that these people are usually very gracious in assisting others who are interested in their areas of expertise. In general, you must express such an interest and be able to display at least a rudimentary knowledge of the subject at hand.

One approach for engaging experts is to provide them with a reference of which they may not be aware. Even better, provide them with an article written by you on the subject. I sometimes ask an expert to comment on one of my articles. This approach provides me with useful criticism and also helps in establishing continuing relationships.

In a study I conducted on fusion energy, I interviewed more than two-dozen of the top experts in the field. Each of these interviews lasted at least an hour and took the people away from other important activities. Before the interviews, however, I made sure that I understood such terms as the deuterium-tritium fuel cycle, a coulomb barrier, and magnet inertia devices. My very basic understanding of these subjects not only made the interviews more valuable, but also helped convince the experts to meet with me.

Another approach for gaining insight from identified experts is to determine if they maintain a blog or contribute regularly to someone else's blog. A search on Google Blog Search, http://www.blogsearch.google.com, for the expert's name or a simple Google search of the expert's name and "blog" should do the trick.

If an expert maintains such a blog, you are likely to pick up many of his or her insights just by following it regularly through the blog's email updates or RSS feeds. (For more on RSS feeds, see http://minitrends.com/blog/what-is-rss.) To engage the expert directly, your meaningful contributions through the comment sections or email, if available, will allow the expert to recognize your interest. This can open the door to future contacts with the expert and others who regularly interact with the site.

Similarly, a Google search with the name of the expert and the word "Twitter" will often find those who have Twitter accounts. Becoming a Twitter follower can be a great way to take advantage of an expert's insights on a continual basis. Often the person or organization that you are following will follow you as a courtesy. This allows you to communicate using a direct tweet to support your building of continuing relationships.

There are also a number of websites in which individuals keep others up-to-date on new business and technology developments via video. Visiting websites such as CNET live, http://cnettv.cnet.com/live/buzz-out-loud, CommandN, http://www.commandn.tv, and Tekzilla, http://revision3 .com/tekzilla, can often suggest interesting Minitrends.

Many colleges conduct special courses for local residents. Participation in such courses is an excellent way to not only keep up to date with developing issues, but also to meet people who can suggest promising Minitrends. For example, the University of Texas at Austin conducts a *Seminars for Adult Growth and Enrichment (SAGE)* program. Recently, I participated in a SAGE course conducted by Dr. John Harrison titled "I Bring You Miracles from the Ether" which discussed the latest developments in on-line social networks.

Dr. Harrison started his academic career as a professor of biochemistry at the University of North Carolina at Chapel Hill. He found he could enhance student learning by utilizing computer-generated models that he shared with colleagues at other university campuses. Because of the success of this program, he was charged by the Chancellor of the university to redesign the Internet system for the University of North Carolina System.

Dr. Harrison was kind enough to meet with me and my book collaborator, Carrie Vanston, to discuss some of the materials he had covered in class. Much of the information and many of the ideas presented in this section were provided by Dr. Harrison.

Maintain Relationships

Communication with knowledgeable people can provide useful input into your search for promising Minitrends. Besides the initial information and insights they provide, they may also be excellent sources for keeping you aware of changing circumstances and new trends. If you successfully initiate a relationship with one or more experts, keeping in contact with these people is important because relationships tend to atrophy rapidly if not exercised. Direct personal or email contact or participation in the social networking techniques previously described can help you to maintain and enhance established relationships.

EXAMINE PATENTS AND PATENT APPLICATIONS

Each year the U.S. Patent and Trademark Office (PTO) issues more than 150,000 patents to companies and individuals throughout the world. Since its establishment in 1790, the PTO has issued almost eight million patents. Of these patents, only about 8% are referred to in any subsequent document such as professional journals, newspaper or magazine articles, conference proceeding, or funding requests. In other words, most patents appear to have had little or no commercial or practical applications.

For an item to be patented, however, it must be "original, nonobvious, and useful." Therefore, any new and useful process, machine, article of manufacture, composition of matter, or distinct variety of plant that has been awarded a patent must have already been screened by PTO for utility and uniqueness. This pre-screening can be quite valuable to anyone seeking to identify Minitrends.

In the U.S., listings of patents granted, patents pending, and disclosure documents can be obtained from the PTO by logging onto http://www.uspto.gov. Obviously, searching through eight million patents is impossible. Restricting your search to patents pending, disclosure documents, or recently granted patents reduces the burden and allows you to focus your effort on current areas that are more relevant to Minitrends. Your search can be further facilitated by the fact that the PTO has classified patents by region, company, filer, and subject areas, such as Electronics, Chemistry, Homes and Fashions, Husbandry, and Industrial Processes.

Most other industrial nations have their own patent offices with similar procedures, objectives, and regulations as the United States PTO. The European Patent Office provides a uniform application procedure for individual inventors and companies seeking patent protection in thirty-eight European countries, http://www.epo.org. Most of these national and international patent offices have working relationships with the U.S. office.

The Battelle Memorial Institute has a long history of patent analysis and is another excellent resource for sifting through the formidable number of patents. Their staff examines trends in patent applications to assist in technology forecasting and business consulting projects. Selected results of their studies can be found on their website, http://www.battelle.org.

REVIEW PH.D. DISSERTATIONS

Every year universities throughout the world award thousands of Doctor of Philosophy degrees in subjects ranging from anthropology and linguistics to science and engineering. For each of the degrees there is a corresponding dissertation, i.e., a document that presents a summary of the author's research and findings. Although these documents vary in quality and usefulness, each is, in theory, a result of a concentrated effort to uncover new information and insights.

Typically, the student is advised on the subject to be investigated by the Chairman of a Dissertation Committee. Usually the subject selected is one in which the Chairman has particular interest and which has not been previously studied in detail. Dissertations often address the forefront of thought in a given subject area and, thus, can provide a special insight into emerging Minitrends.

ProQuest, Inc., http://www.proquest.com, records and organizes dissertations in a number of categories. The service lists more than two million entries, and the number of documents in each subject area is often very large. Searching these catalogues efficiently requires some type of rational plan. Such a plan might be based on author, subject area, university, geography, or dissertation committee members.

> As I prepared this book, a colleague suggested that I investigate "Cloud Computing" as a Minitrend. Cloud Computing is a system in which most computation and data storage is done at a facility remote from the base computer. To check this out, I requested a list of dissertations on the subject from ProQuest and found a dissertation on the subject by a student at Georgia Tech from 2008. While I was at it, I checked on my own dissertation on fusion power for the University of Texas at Austin and found that, yes, it was recorded on the list.

Another excellent source, and one which many libraries are going to in addition to or instead of ProQuest, is the Networked Digital Library of Theses and Dissertations, http://www.ndltd.org. This international organization is dedicated to promoting the adoption, creation, use, dissemination and preservation of electronic analogues to the traditional paper-based theses and dissertations.

PAY HEED TO TELEVISION

Studies indicate that the average American watches television an average of three-and-a- half hours a day. This indicates that our television sets provide us with one of our greatest sources of information and ideas. News broadcasts, personal interviews, special Public Broadcasting System programs, and public debates can often suggest the emergence of promising Minitrends. Even dramas and comedies designed primarily for entertainment can hint at emerging social trends. A decade ago, leading characters in many TV programs were typically shown with a cigarette in one hand and a martini in another. This is no longer true. In the same timeframe, major parts for minority players were rare, but this has been steadily changing.

There are currently almost 300 television networks operating in the United States, as well as hundreds of networks operating in other countries throughout the world. Several of these networks, such as NBC, CBS, ABC, Fox, and PBS, target general audiences, but most focus on special interests such as children, sports enthusiasts, gender groups, and political junkies. Many networks offer programming rich in content that can suggest possible Minitrends. These include, but are not limited to, the Discovery Channel, the History Channel, the Science Channel, the National Geographic Channel, and the Smithsonian Channel. Programs on channels such as these can not only suggest Minitrends, but are entertaining as well.

One further suggestion: If a television program fires a Minitrend synapse in your brain, it can well be forgotten as other subjects and ideas are presented. I advise you to keep a note pad, portable recorder, PDA, or other electronic recording device handy to record the thought as it occurs.

EXAMINE THE PLATFORMS OF LOSING PRESIDENTIAL CANDIDATES

In the conduct of political elections, particularly the ones for president, issues raised by the loser often have new life after the election. For example, during his 1956 campaign for president, one of Adlai Stevenson's platforms was the establishment of an international Nuclear Test Ban Treaty, a position that contributed to his defeat. In time, however, the idea increased in popularity and on August 5, 1963, representatives of the United States, the USSR, and the United Kingdom signed such a treaty. The U.S. Senate ratified the treaty by a vote of 80 to 19, and it entered into force on October 10, 1963.

In the 1964 presidential election, Senator Barry Goldwater, running on a conservative platform, was soundly defeated by Lyndon Johnson. However, the platform on which he ran laid the groundwork that paved the way for the Ronald Reagan revolution.

In the 2000 presidential election, one of Al Gore's key issues was global climate change. On his defeat, this issue faded from public attention for several years. However, by 2006 it had became a matter of widespread concern as troubling consequences became increasingly well recognized—and Al Gore received an Academy Award, a Grammy Award, an Emmy Award, and a Nobel Peace Prize for his work in this area.

Most people pay little attention to the ideas of a losing candidate, but examination of these ideas can provide indications of Minitrends to come.

ALL VERY INTERESTING, BUT FRANKLY, SO WHAT?

In searching for emerging Minitrends, you must combine curiosity and openness of mind with a discipline that ensures ideas are carefully examined, considered, and recorded. Good ideas must be carefully nourished. As I discuss in subsequent chapters, in time you will have to select the specific Minitrends and specific applications of those trends on which to concentrate. Later, it will be necessary for you to determine how you will translate a selected Minitrend into a practical business application. The information that you collect and analyze in the searching phase will prove very useful as you undertake these tasks.

In this chapter and the previous one, I address the principles involved in identifying and analyzing Minitrends. In Chapters Four, Five, and Six I demonstrate how these principles can be applied in the cases of nine specific Minitrends. In each case, I examine the Minitrend in terms of Background, Current Trends, and Business Opportunities.

For each of the Minitrends discussed in these chapters I indicate my initial introduction to the trend. You will note that in most cases the source of this introduction was a suggestion by a friend or acquaintance, an article that I saw in a newspaper or magazine, or a meeting or conference I attended.

I believe each of these Minitrends promise to become significant within the next few years. The primary purpose of the chapters, however, is to provide you with guidance on how you can define the business opportunities resident in Minitrends that you, yourself, uncover.

Part III: Some Attractive Minitrends

Examining how others uncovered and profited from precious gems can enlighten gem seekers. Likewise, demonstrating the practical application of Minitrends analysis and the resulting business opportunities can offer you insights for conducting your own Minitrend analysis.

Chapter Four

Minitrends for Individuals

In Chapters Two and Three, I discuss some techniques for uncovering emerging Minitrends and some sources for gathering information that can be used in employing these techniques. In this chapter and the following two, I examine nine Minitrends that I believe offer interesting business opportunities and demonstrate how you can conduct your own Minitrend analyses.

I hope the discussions of these Minitrends provide information and insights that prove useful to you. The primary objective of these chapters, however, is to provide you with guidelines you can use to uncover and analyze your own Minitrends. In this regard, at the end of each Minitrend, I explain how I became aware of and interested in that trend.

In this chapter, I examine three Minitrends I believe could be particularly valuable to individuals or small groups of individuals (up to about six) who are interested in launching new enterprises. In Chapter Five, I discuss three Minitrends that I believe could be particularly valuable to executives of small and middle-size companies who are interested in new approaches for improving their businesses or introducing new product lines. In Chapter Six, I analyze three Minitrends I believe could be particularly valuable to large companies interested in identifying new business opportunities.

For each of these Minitrends, I discuss the background of the subject, current trends, and some of the business opportunities offered by the Minitrend. Although each of the three chapters focuses on a particular business group, all nine of the Minitrends discussed in these chapters offer potential opportunities to all three groups.

EXPANDING INVOLVEMENT IN VIRTUAL WORLDS

Background

Virtual worlds are computer-based platforms that allow participants to engage in a wide range of real-world type activities such as buying virtual world property, building and furnishing virtual world homes and offices, producing and selling virtual world goods, virtual traveling, taking part in virtual world social activities such as parties and fundraisers, and communicating and having meetings with other participants. The virtual world concept grew out of alternate reality games in which the story is developed by participants' decisions and actions. Virtual world platforms, however, are not really games, since there are no scores, no winners or losers, and no game endings. Although the individuals and organizations that originate and manage the platforms establish ground rules and exercise some control over platform activities, in most virtual worlds, platform participants generate the bulk of program content.

There are a number of virtual world platforms available, and new ones are constantly being developed. A recent report by *Virtual World Review* listed twenty-nine platforms classified by types, e.g., by age groups, by experience with programs, and by ways to access the virtual world. Each platform has its own rules, characteristics, and special features. Currently, the most popular platform is "Second Life," initiated and operated by Linden Laboratories, Inc. (The volatility of virtual worlds is reflected by the discontinuation on March 9, 2010 of "There," formerly the second most popular platform.)

To participate in a virtual world platform, a user creates an "avatar," a 2D or 3D computerized representation of himself or herself with a related name or "handle." The avatar can be a person, an animal, an imaginary creature, or even an inanimate object. Depending on the specific platform involved, the avatar can be distinguished by sex, age, physical characteristics, and clothing. (Younger users tend to be very imaginative in developing their avatars, while older users tend to select avatars with characteristics similar to their own.) Some platforms allow users to display emotions ("emotes" or "smileys"), such as happiness, sadness, gratitude, or uncertainty.

Recent developments in platforms include "text to speech" technology that allows an avatar to actually speak in chatting sessions and "dynamic avatars" in which limited physical activities can be preprogrammed. Users are not restricted to a single avatar in each world but can develop multiple identities and even interact with themselves. In most platforms, avatars can travel easily by teleportation, foot, helicopters, hot air balloons, submarines, and even special user-conceived vehicles.

Most platforms have in-world currencies. For example, Second Life utilizes Lindendollars (L$). Users can acquire these virtual world currencies by purchasing them in real world currencies from the platform manager, by borrowing from virtual world banks, or from sales or rent from other users. The value of these virtual world currencies varies depending on in-world circumstances. However, platform managers sometimes act as a central bank to maintain some stability in the currency. At present, the value of an L$ is about .004 U.S. dollars which makes it slightly more valuable than a Japanese Yen.

One important activity in many platforms is buying real estate and building structures on the property. In the Active Worlds platform, there are over 1,000 active building worlds to build on and tens of thousands of builds. AlphaWorld, Active Worlds' largest public building world, has more available building space than the real-world State of California (but without the taxes).

Current trends

Although virtual worlds emerged on the market a number of years ago (Active Worlds was launched in 1995 and Second Life in 2003), the industry is still in a transformational stage.

The exact size of the market is difficult to determine. There are, however, strong indications that the market is growing. For example, Second Life reported 9.8 million registered accounts in 2006, and 13 million in 2008. In 2010, Second Life reportedly reached 20 million accounts.

In addition to the growth in registered accounts, continuous enhancements are being developed. In September 2008, the Merl company launched a beta test of a social network that integrates nineteen virtual world platforms to meet the desire of users to coordinate lives in different worlds. Although full integration is currently limited for some platforms, the goal is to bring together the different virtual worlds and create an integrated virtual world system.

In July 2008, Linden Lab announced that it had successfully "teleported" avatars into a virtual world operated by IBM. Interoperability between different virtual worlds, each of which has its own proprietary software and unique program, is expected to greatly enhance the attractiveness of the concept. It might be noted that this project only teleported the avatars themselves and not their clothing. The avatars arrived in their new world as gray, nude-like forms, which may have caused them some embarrassment.

Another important trend is the growing porosity between the virtual world and the real world and the increasing capacity of users to move smoothly between the two.

A significant trend in the virtual world environment is the increasing use of these worlds for practical purposes. A number of commercial organizations are evaluating virtual worlds for product advertisements, new product testing, identification of new markets, uncovering unexpected problems with new marketing programs, and other commercial purposes. Such tasks can often be performed in virtual worlds much faster, cheaper, and with less risk than traditional marketing programs.

As an indication of the seriousness with which many participants take their virtual lives, in Tokyo, Japan recently, a 43 year-old piano teacher, shocked by the fact that her virtual husband divorced her without warning or reason, logged on with his platform ID and password (that he gave her during the happy times of their "marriage") and murdered her virtual spouse. In the real-world, she has been charged with illegally accessing a computer and manipulating electronic data and faces a five-year prison sentence or a fine of up to $5,000. Whether or not she will be tried for murder in the virtual world, and, if so, whom she will hire as a lawyer is not known.

A particularly interesting and practical use of virtual world capabilities is in the educational arena, where they are being used for simulation, research, performance, design, collaboration, and communication. The technology is proving particularly valuable in distance learning environments. A number of colleges and universities have found that use of virtual worlds allows more meaningful interaction between students and teachers located in different areas. Virtual worlds can also allow better tailoring of instructional material to individual students.

Major colleges and universities using virtual worlds to support their educational programs include the University of Florida, Rice University, the University of Texas in Austin, Vassar College, Harvard University, Stanford University, University College Dublin, the University of Edinburgh, Delft University of Technology, and the Hong Kong Polytechnic University. To support such programs, Second Life has established an "archipelago" of education-focused islands.

> To assist students and others in learning about art and architecture, Vassar College has constructed a Second Life version of Michelangelo's Sistine Chapel. In this recreation, the interior is depicted in great detail, while the exterior is an approximation. Participants can fly up to the top of a wall for a close inspection, look down at the inlaid floor, or even sit on a window ledge! The lower tier of the chapel normally displays panels with painted draperies. On special occasions, these panels are covered with tapestries designed by Raphael. You can click to show or hide the tapestries whenever you want.

The Educators Coop, a community of university faculty members, librarians, and K-12 teachers from thirty-two educational institutions, recently conducted a Second Life research project to examine how use of virtual world platforms can impact the professional and personal lives of participants. Results from the first six-month phase of the project indicate that using the platform allows professionals to collaborate productively with other members of their profession.

One education arena generating interest is language learning. In fact, there are several platforms, such as Zon and Wiz

World, specifically developed for this purpose. Moreover, replication of cities such as Barcelona, Berlin, London, or Paris permit students to practice new languages through virtual tourism, while engaged in more traditional learning activities, such as classroom instruction and special projects.

As an example of the increasing use of virtual worlds in new applications, the U.S. Air Force is planning to give all new recruits Second Life virtual world avatars from the moment they are accepted into the military service. These avatars will remain with the airmen and airwomen throughout their careers. It will travel with them, grow with them, change appearance with them. It will provide them a history of where they've been and a notion of where they're going. In their virtual world lives, they will also be able to take classes, review materials, perform pre-deployment exercises, and tour facilities.

Business opportunities

In an arena as growing and dynamic as virtual world, the number of potential business opportunities is almost endless.

The most obvious opportunities for qualified individuals and small companies are those associated with software development. Although developing a new virtual world is expensive and requires a great deal of time and effort, the existing worlds are very amenable to new software that can add new features and capabilities to their existing worlds, e.g., platform add-ons that reduce computer memory and processing requirements, reduce the learning curve for participants, and make the worlds more accessible to new markets.

All of the virtual world platforms are interested in adding users to their systems, and individuals and groups who can assist in this goal will be attractive to their real-world executives. Software modifications and add-ons are often developed by small groups (two to six people) with little available capital. People interested in defining industry requirements and identifying possible business opportunities are well-advised to attend an annual *Virtual Worlds Conference* or obtain conference proceedings.

As indicated in the Current Trends section, many commercial organizations are evaluating virtual worlds for advertising effectiveness and market testing for new or reintroduced products and services. There will be needs for groups that understand how virtual worlds can be utilized for these purposes and how results from such activities can be properly evaluated. In similar manner, education and library organizations may be interested in assistance from knowledgeable virtual world experts in visualizing, conceptualizing, and formulating methods and techniques that will increase the value of the platforms.

Although most people are capable of participating in simple virtual world activities, many users may wish to enhance their skills for more complicated tasks, such as developing creative avatars, more complex buildings, or more attractive furniture, landscapes, vehicles, etc. Virtual world experts may be used to either instruct novices in more complicated procedures or, perhaps, assist them in utilizing the capabilities of the worlds more effectively.

Users can use the graphic, animation, and sound tools of the virtual world to cheaply design buildings, furniture, clothing, and art objects that can then be transferred into the real world and sold for profit. Many of the platforms have features specifically designed to assist writers and artists in developing unique and novel products. These tools may also prove attractive to those in the fast-paced fashion industry. Some platforms allow users to retain rights to objects designed on the system.

Because users are able to sell virtual world currencies to other users for real world money, astute traders can actually accrue real incomes from virtual world activities. Linden Lab has reported that in February 2009, 233 users had made profits of more than $5,000 and a few users have grossed in excess of a million dollars per year from Second Life transactions.

Although most users are fortunate to earn enough money to meet virtual world expenses, there is always room for people with special skills and aptitudes to make real world money in the make-believe world.

Discovery process: Although I was vaguely aware of the existence of the Second Life platform, I considered it basically an escape mechanism for people who didn't have a First Life. I became aware of the potential impact of virtual world activities at a lecture by Dr. Leslie Jarmon at the University of Texas at Austin. Later, I corresponded with Dr. Jarmon by email. She gave me additional information about current developments, sent me copies of two articles on the subject that she was submitting for publication, and reviewed an earlier version of the material included in this section.

SUPPORT FOR PEOPLE WORKING AT HOME

Background

The cost, time, and effort involved in commuting, the cost of child care, supportive business practices, an increasing number of very small businesses, and personal preferences have resulted in a steady growth in the number of individuals working part-time or full-time at home over the last two decades. It is estimated that as much as twenty-five percent of all white collar work is now being done in private residences.

Although individuals and organizations have found a number of advantages in at-home employment, they have also found many disadvantages in the practice. At-home workers often find that:

- They miss the advantages of having people immediately available to discuss ideas, suggest new approaches, assist in communication, and provide moral support.

- They often do not have facilities and equipment, such as color printers, high-speed copiers, meeting spaces, snack bars, etc., that are typically available in central offices.

- Administrative support for typing, filing, editing, and budgeting is not available.

- Teaming with co-workers often proves difficult when face-to-face communications are impractical.

In addition to these practical disadvantages, people working at home often find that they miss the comradeship and intellectual stimulation found in central offices, find many distractions to their work, and may find it difficult to exercise the discipline required to maintain a suitable work schedule when there is no structure to their day's activities.

Current trends

To overcome the disadvantages of work-at-home employment, a number of informal or semi-formal activities are emerging. Starbucks coffee bars were an early solution for providing informal settings for people to work or conduct meetings. Although these coffee bars have been useful for many people, they have the disadvantages of often being crowded, noisy, and distracting. Moreover, they provide few support facilities, and there is a limit to how long people can comfortably remain in the establishment.

A number of solutions are emerging to better meet the needs and desires of people working at home, These include: small offices or meeting rooms that can be rented by the day or even by the hour; chat rooms where people can meet informally to discuss ideas; semiformal groups that meet regularly to establish person-to-person interactions; and temporary support staffs to provide administrative assistance as needed.

Considering the driving forces listed in the Background section, it appears likely that the fraction of people working at home will continue to grow. As a result, the need for support services and facilities—and the market for providing them—will also grow for the foreseeable future.

Business opportunities

The activities discussed under Current Trends tend to be low-effort, low-cost projects with little capital investment requirements. Such projects can be easily initiated by those clever enough to understand the market and take advantage of its growth. In fact, people working at home may tailor their efforts to support not only their own businesses, but also to serve other businesses at a profit.

Most individuals and groups that have established businesses to support at-home workers are small and locally focused. There is an increasing amount of interaction, however, between individual support groups to exchange ideas, promote cooperation, and enhance marketing. A potential market for such businesses could also be larger companies that wish to provide support for their home-workers, much as they currently provide childcare. In fact, companies may wish to provide childcare for work-at-home employees to increase their productivity.

In June 2008, two Rice University graduate students, Ned Dodington and Matthew Wettergreen, opened Caroline Collective, LLC, a co-working space company in Houston, Texas. Caroline Collective provides a wide range of talented professionals with a relaxed working environment of the home office combined with a dynamic social atmosphere. The company provides private and shared offices, conference and meeting rooms, shower facilities, and exhibition space, as well as WiFi, coffee, and snacks. The clients represent a variety of creative artists, writers, and other professionals. The 6000 square-foot space is located in Houston's dynamic Museum District and is reported to currently be the largest co-space in the world. All of the company's working space was rented before it opened, and the company reports a steadily growing community of regular dedicated members and drop-ins.

There are currently dozens of "co-working" groups throughout the world. As with many service-providing businesses, groups who succeed in such businesses may well decide to expand by franchising programs as McDonald's, Starbucks, and a host of other chains have done successfully. Such expansions could well result from consolidations of established small firms.

Discovery process: Austin, Texas has long been known for its interest and support of entrepreneurial individuals, as evidenced by the Austin Technology Incubator supported by the University of Texas at Austin. Over the years, a number of my colleagues have started small businesses, many working initially from their homes. (In fact, this is the way I launched Technology Futures, Inc.) In addition to the start-up businesses that needed support, I have been acquainted with a number of artists, musicians, accountants, lawyers, etc., who could also use administrative assistance. Based on my experience and that of friends, it appeared there was a need for the types of services described above. I, therefore, began to search for organizations that supplied such support and found that it was a small but growing market.

EXPANDING CAPABILITIES OF ADVANCED WEBSITES

Background

The World Wide Web was developed during the period 1989-1990 by Sir Tim Berners-Lee, a British scientist at the European Organization for Nuclear Research (CERN). The key element in the Web concept was the marrying of hypertext technology with the Internet. (Hypertext is a technology that automatically connects one piece of information with other related information, e.g., texts, pictures, music, videos.) Originally, the Web was intended to support the efficient transfer of information between scientists and scientific groups.

In 1991, the Web was released to the public on a free, non-proprietary basis. An important characteristic of the Web is that the user can request information directly from its owner without permission or notification. The non-proprietary nature of the Web means that servers and clients can be developed independently without licensing restrictions. In 1993, the Mosaic Web browser was introduced that added video content, animation, and rich Graphical User Interface (GUI) features to the platform, markedly increasing Web attractiveness.

The Web consists of all publicly accessible websites containing data, graphs, photographs, videos, and/or other digital assets. These are accessed by a globally unique domain name known as its "Uniform Resource Locator" (URL), which is assigned by an accredited domain name registrar.

Users can identify relevant websites with "search engines" by entering key words or phrases. Search engines store very large bodies of information—texts, charts, and graphics— typically gathered from the Web itself. In the late 1990s, search engine technology was advanced by the development of a computer algorithm that allows an almost infinite number of websites to be automatically indexed.

There are a very large number of search engines available for either general usage or special purpose employment, e.g., medical information, legal documentation, employment searches, and geographic representation. One recent study identified more than 2,000 search engines located in 120 different countries. Popular general usage search engines include Yahoo, Ask, and, easily the most widely used, Google (which had 63% of U.S. searches in August 2008). Since its introduction, use of the Web has grown dramatically. In 2008 there were more than 100 million websites in operation, 11.5 billion pages of indexable Web pages available, and one trillion unique domain names. In 2009, Microsoft announced a new search engine named "Bing" to replace its previous search engine, "Live Search." The new search engine is designed to compete directly with Google.

Although the Web has proven to be extremely popular, there were many users who believed that the traditional Web structure, i.e., one that was limited to users querying a search engine that contained potentially useful information, did not take advantage of the Web itself as a platform. These users were convinced the Web could serve as a mechanism for promoting the exchange of information, ideas, and insights among Web users. Such a platform would be characterized by (1) interaction between information users and information providers, (2) user participation in Web activities, (3) information socialization, and (4) utilization of the combined intelligence of all website participants.

At a website conference in 2004, Tim O'Reilly coined the term Web 2.0 to characterize this approach to Web usage. (Previous Web approaches were retroactively referred to as Web 1.0.) Although the definition of Web 2.0 varies between individuals and appears to change over time, the key concepts involve extensive involvement of users, interconnectivity between users, lightweight business models, flexibility, and ease of use.

To accomplish these goals, Web 2.0 participants use such activities as wikis (Web pages in which any user can add new information or modify or elaborate on old information), "blogs" (websites, usually maintained by individuals, that allow for the creation, editing, and distribution of information, opinions, videos, music, etc.), and "Internet forums" (communities of Web users designed to support discussions between participants and introduce new information and ideas). As an indication of the popularity of such activities, BlogPulse recently tracked 126 million blogs on the Internet.

Web 2.0 technologies have led to the establishment of hundreds of "Social Network Sites (SNS)" with millions of users. These websites can be characterized in two categories. Members of the first group, such as MySpace, Facebook, and MyFace, focus primarily on social interactions, such as identifying and engaging new friends, renewing old friendships, and communicating with social contacts. Members of the second group, such as LinkedIn and Plaxo, concentrate more on establishing and maintaining business contacts. Many SNSs are structured to appeal to particular professions, geographical areas, or special interests. (See also "Social Networking Platforms" in Chapter Three.)

Current trends

The limited control of information and ideas contributed by users is one of the problems inherent in the open nature of Web 2.0 procedures. Individual users may have little or no knowledge about the subject they are commenting on, and in some cases, contributors may have ulterior motives to provide incorrect or misleading information. The basic theory of wikis, forums, and blogs is that the wisdom of the group of contributors will, in time, correct any misinformation that is produced. In many cases, of course, this doesn't prove to be true. Users of the outputs of these programs may not be totally confident of their correctness.

Many wikis have introduced "referees" to evaluate or corroborate user input in order to minimize the probability of incorrect information being presented. Most forums have some type of moderator to not only guide group discussions, but also to provide some overview of the soundness of provided information. These referees and moderators, however, restrict the openness and informality associated with Web 2.0. Currently, Web 2.0 users are creating and testing new techniques to minimize questionable input while maintaining the freedom of Web 2.0.

Just as Web 2.0 is building on the existing Web structure to establish more interactive platforms, a number of interested parties are working to add new capabilities to the Web. The combination of these new capabilities and technological approaches, representing the third generation of the Web, is often referred to as Web 3.0. This term was coined by John Markin in 2006 and is sometimes referred to as the "Intelligent Web."

As is the case with Web 2.0, there are different definitions of Web 3.0, different opinions on its purposes and goals, and different projections of how long it will take the technology to deliver on its promises. In general terms, Web 3.0 can be characterized as the substitution of computer activities for human activities, particularly activities that are repetitive, burdensome, and uninteresting. From a practical standpoint, Web 3.0 is not a single technology or capability, but rather a group of emerging technical advances that promise to provide a wide range of capabilities. (An interesting differentiation between the different Web platforms is offered by Reed Hastings, one of the founders of Netflix, "Web 1.0 was dial up, 50 kilobit average bandwidth; Web 2.0 is, on average, one megabit, part time; Web 3.0 will be 10 megabits, full time.")

Research on Web 3.0 is continuing, and new advances are being reported each year. However, the argument can be made that Web 3.0 represents not a final product, but rather a series of intermediate products, leading eventually to effective artificial intelligence that can interact with humans in natural language.

Business opportunities

Because of the turbulent activity in both Web 2.0 and Web 3.0, there are almost unlimited opportunities for qualified individuals to develop new software that can increase the power and utility of each platform. In fact, Yahoo has, in a recent new product announcement, specifically asked third-party developers to create services that can be run on its new home page.

Examples of people who have successfully created business opportunities in the Web area include:

- Ward Cummingham, who initiated the "wiki" concept in 1995

- Larry Page and Sergey Brin, who launched Google in 1997 while students at Stanford University

- Tom Anderson and Chris DeWolfe, who began MySpace in 2003

- Mark Zuckerberg, who founded Facebook in 2004 while still a student at Harvard University

- Chad Hurley, Steve Chen, and Jawed Karim, who launched YouTube in 2005

Taking full advantage of different programs and technologies associated with Web 2.0 and Web 3.0 requires knowledge, experience, and imagination. People with these qualifications will be in demand as both consultants and educators for individuals and organizations desiring to utilize the power of these platforms. One of the most interesting developments in the Web 2.0 and Web 3.0 arenas is the use of the platforms for marketing and advertising purposes. Processes for utilizing the power of the platforms effectively are now being developed, and imaginative people who can develop, initiate, manage, and evaluate such processes will have opportunities that are both interesting and profitable.

Familiarity with continuing developments in Web technology and usage will provide both small and large companies with the ability to gain competitive advantages over competitors who fail to appreciate the power of these new developments in terms of better communications with current and potential customers, better access to knowledge sources and forefront thinking, and early application of machine learning techniques. These advantages can lead to the identification and exploitation of very attractive new business possibilities.

Discovery process: I first became aware of the recent advances in the Web at a presentation at a World Futures Society meeting by David Armistead and Jon Lebkowsky of Strategic Web Associates, LLC. After the WFS meeting, I discussed their comments with them and set up a meeting with Mr. Armistead in which he brought me up to date on current Web developments. He also suggested that I get in contact with Kavita Patel of the Pluck Corporation, who was kind enough to give me additional information and to review this section of the book.

ALL VERY INTERESTING, BUT FRANKLY, SO WHAT?

In this chapter, I examine three Minitrends I find interesting and that I believe offer promising business opportunities. You will note that each of these examples meets the basic criteria for a Minitrend.

- Each one has advanced to the stage where development will probably continue and where you can make reasonable projections of key milestones, the time it will take to reach these milestones, and where the trend will eventfully lead.

- In each case there appears to be a high probability that the trend will be of significant importance within the next five years.

- It does not appear that the trend is well-recognized or appreciated by the general public or most business leaders.

In regard to the last criterion, there are, of course, people and organizations that do recognize these trends and some may have already invested in their development. If this were not true, the trends wouldn't be emerging. However, my discussions with a broad range of individuals and business leaders indicate that few have more than a vague knowledge of the trends, and even fewer have detailed familiarity with the subject area.

For each listed Minitrend, I have indicated how I became interested in the subject. Looking over these "discovery process" sections, you will note a repeated pattern. In each case, I had a fuzzy awareness of the trend to start with. Later, the importance of the subject was brought to my attention by a friend, a presentation at a meeting or conference, or an article in a formal publication.

Once I appreciated the importance of a Minitrend, I began a more detailed examination of the background of the trend. In studying the backgrounds, I made extensive use of the sources listed in Chapter Three. As I suggest in the "Establish Social Networks" section in that chapter, I talked with a number of experts in each Minitrend area. This not only added special insights into the subject area, but also introduced me to new friends who keep me updated on changes in the areas involved.

I expect that your search for attractive Minitrends will follow a similar pattern:

- A vague recognition of the trend

- Preliminary evaluation of the trend to determine its potential

- A more detailed analysis of the trend

- A definition of possible business opportunities

I should mention that even a preliminary analysis of a Minitrend involves a considerable amount of time and effort, even after the subject has been selected. Because of the time and effort required for analyses, you must be careful in your selection of the Minitrends you choose to examine.

In the final section of each Minitrend, I discuss the potential business opportunities for individuals, small and medium-size businesses, and large businesses. I do this to indicate that there are attractive opportunities for each of these groups. However, since this chapter is intended to focus primarily on business opportunities for individuals and small groups of individuals, I paid particular attention to this group. In Chapter Five, I focus on Minitrends that are particularly relevant to small and medium-size businesses and, in Chapter Six, I discuss Minitrends of particular relevance to large companies.

As you examine Minitrends you might wish to exploit, considering any situation other than your own is not necessary or even appropriate. If you are an individual or member of a small group of individuals, the Minitrends that could provide an opportunity for starting a new business will probably be of most interest. If you are part of a small or medium-sized business, possible new business areas that may be opened by Minitrends will probably be of most interest. If you are employed by a large company, you will probably be most interested in Minitrends that may lead either to acquisition of smaller companies or the establishment of new business areas in your company.

The point is that while I examined business opportunities for a range of individuals and companies, you will only have to concentrate on those relevant to your particular situation.

Chapter Five

Minitrends for Small and Medium-Size Companies

In Chapter One, I classify the groups who might benefit from exploiting Minitrends into three categories:

- Individuals or small groups of individuals

- Large companies that have revenues of at least $200 million per year, or have 50,000 or more employees

- Small and medium-size companies that fall between the two other categories

The last group includes companies that vary widely in size, products and services, geographic location, history, and culture. Most of these companies, however, share one characteristic—they are constantly challenged for their long-term success or even existence. These challenges include:

- Diminishing need and/or market for their product or services

- Competition from similar companies that offer comparable products or services at a lower price, with greater capabilities, or more attractive features

- Competition from larger companies that can take advantage of economies of scale

To survive such challenges, small and medium-size companies must be constantly searching for ways to decrease costs, increase capabilities, and add attractive features. Achieving these objectives may involve more efficient production approaches, better distribution and service procedures, more effective marketing programs, or improvements in their own products or services. All of these goals can be served through, appropriate utilization of Minitrends.

In determining the types of Minitrends that could bolster companies of this size, consideration of the characteristics of the group is very useful. These companies typically have established product lines, customer bases, operating procedures, and knowledgeable employees. They normally have sufficient personnel, equipment, facilities, and funds to support a fair amount of product development and market research and are able to wait a reasonable amount of time for markets to clarify. They also, however, tend to be somewhat risk adverse.

These companies are well positioned to take advantage of promising Minitrends if there are reasonable prospects of success within two to five years. The three Minitrends I examine in this chapter have such prospects. As I note in Chapter Four, however, the examples presented are intended primarily to demonstrate a process for analyzing Minitrends.

INCREASED INTEREST IN PRIVACY

Background

The modern concept of privacy is relatively new. In earlier days, when most of the population lived in villages, everyone in the village was well aware of the personal and business activities of their neighbors, and people outside the village didn't know, or care, about these activities.

As our society became more centralized, sophisticated, and complex, people became more guarded about their backgrounds, relationships, and actions. Most citizens chose to be "left alone" and not open their private lives to scrutiny.

Two recent trends have called this privacy concept into question. First, maintaining individual privacy has become increasingly difficult because of advances in technology. Second, many people are showing an increasing willingness to make details of their private lives more open to others. Although there are many facets to the privacy concept, most can be categorized into the areas of messaging, personal profiling, and identity. (Although security is related to privacy, in this section I address that subject only to the extent that it affects personal privacy. Likewise, I give no attention to business privacy which is basically a different subject area.)

Messaging

The development and widespread expansion of the Internet dramatically changed the nature of communications throughout the world. Individuals can now easily send documents, photographs, videos, and personal messages to others anywhere on the globe. This capability enables the conduct of financial transactions, the sharing of information and ideas, and the maintenance and strengthening of personal and family bonds.

The increasing use of the Internet, however, has been accompanied by the development of a variety of tools that allow hackers to gain access to personal information. These tools include:

- *Trojan Horse*—a malicious, security-breaking program typically installed on a computer as the result of the downloading of some attractive feature such as free merchandise or useful data. Once installed, the program remains unknown to the user but is capable of sending key data to unauthorized recipients.

- *Phishing*—an attack that provides an attacker with information, such as user names, passwords, and PIN numbers, that provide access credentials to attackers.

- *Pharming*—an attack that redirects messages from its intended addressee to a bogus website that allows an attacker to receive unauthorized information.

- *Man-in-the-Middle*—an attack in which an attacker surreptitiously interjects his or her messages into communications between two attacked parties.

- *Spyware*—computer software installed surreptitiously on a personal computer to collect information about users, their computers, and/or their browsing habits without the user's informed consent.

There is software available to counter each of these privacy-invasive tools. However, to counter them it is necessary to be aware of this software and to use it properly.

Personal profiles

As we go through our daily lives, each of us leaves numerous clues about who we are, whom we deal with, what we prefer, and in what activities we are involved. These clues may involve transactions in which we are involved, purchases we make, cell phone and Internet messages, photographs on security cameras, and travel agendas based on RFID (Radio Frequency Identifier) transmissions. Each of these clues may tell something about you which you may or may not want others to know. Recent developments in data fusion programs that combine and correlate individual clues, now allow others to formulate a very complete profile of you as an individual. (The gambling casinos throughout the world have been on the forefront of data fusion for some time.)

Obviously, the more information a person provides and the larger the number of people and organizations to whom the information is provided, the more detailed that profile can be. With the increasing popularity and pervasiveness of social networks such as Facebook, MySpace, YouTube, and LinkedIn, many individuals are providing others with more details about their personal lives than was normal in the past. Most of these common social networks have incorporated safeguards. However, the reality is that, given the structure of the Internet and the ambiguities of human nature, supposedly confidential information often becomes available to those for whom it was not intended.

"Sexting," the practice of sending sexually explicit text and photos of oneself or others, most commonly by the use of cell phones, is becoming popular among some younger people. This is an extreme example of the phenomenon of making personal matter available to others. Since the practice is most common among teenagers, there have been cases where either the person sending photos or the person receiving photos has been charged as a sex offender. There has been at least one case of suicide by a girl whose revealing photo message to a boyfriend was spread throughout her school.

As sexting has become more common, parents, school officials, and government agencies have become increasingly concerned about the practice.

Identity

Although unauthorized distribution of personal information may be troubling and embarrassing, the greatest privacy threat to individuals is "identity theft." Such theft can result in significant monetary loss, damage to reputation, and considerable inconvenience. It is highly important for individuals to take strong precautions to prevent its occurrence. Although there are a number of ways by which offenders can gain personal information, the most common method is by use of the Internet hacking tools like those listed in the previous section. Precautions that can be taken to prevent identify theft include passwords (or passphrases), virus checks, and careful adherence to best privacy practices.

The most commonly used technique for protecting private information is the use of passwords. The user formulates some series of letters, numbers, and symbols that is made available to a website with which communications is desired. The user may provide the site with various personal data. To recover this data, the user must present the proper password to the site. In general, the longer and more complicated the password is, the more secure the data will be. In practice, many sites specify the minimum length and complexity of a password. For example, one government agency requires that passwords be at least eight characters long and include at least one number, one symbol, one lower case letter, and one upper case letter.

Although the password approach can be very useful in protecting private data, in reality, many people compromise the power of the technique by using the same password for multiple sites, writing down passwords, selecting easily deciphered passwords such as special dates, addresses, or phone numbers, and providing passwords to others indiscriminately. (The government agency cited above, noting the difficulty of remembering complex passwords, suggested that users formulate easily remembered combinations, such as ICU8a#@9 (I see you ate a pound at nine). Such a practice, of course, diminishes the power of the password.)

When the Social Security Act of 1935 was passed, each worker was assigned a Social Security Number (SSN). By statute, the use of this number was limited to Social Security activities. As time has passed, however, the number has become the most common means of personal identification. Currently, many groups such as banks, credit card suppliers, and retail sales outlets require that they be provided with the number in order to conduct transactions. Thus, its role in privacy protection is increasingly limited.

In many cases, organizations request only the last four digits of the SSN for identification in Internet transactions. Providing this information reduces the protection provided by the number by a factor of ten thousand. Moreover, because of the process the government uses to assign SSNs, it is reasonably simple for offenders to determine the other five digits if they can determine where and when the person was born.

Current trends

In a 2008 presentation at a *Last HOPE Conference*, Steven Rambam, director of the Pallorium investigative agency, made the proclamation that "Privacy is dead—get over it." This position has been accepted by a number of other knowledgeable people. The basic premise of this position is that technology has advanced to the point where completely protecting private information is virtually impossible. People, should accept that fact and act accordingly.

Although there is a considerable amount of truth in this position, in the last couple of years many individuals and groups have become increasingly concerned about this problem and are seeking methods to better protect their privacy. As an indication of this trend, the Scientific American magazine devoted its entire September 2008 issue to threats to privacy and steps that could taken to minimize these threats. The truth is that there are techniques for countering invasions of privacy available to the public. Until recently, however, most people have not availed themselves of these techniques.

There are three approaches to protecting personal information from compromise—personal caution, technology aids, and group action.

Personal caution

Undoubtedly, the most common sources of personal information disclosure are the individuals themselves. In daily life, there are an almost unlimited range of organizations requesting information such as addresses, phone and fax numbers, email addresses, annual income, date and place of birth, current and previous employers, and personal relationships. For reasons of convenience and savings, many people provide such information with little resistance or complaint. Although these pieces of information may not, in themselves, be particularly revealing, in these days of data fusion they may provide a very comprehensive picture of who you are, what you like, what you have done in the past, and with whom you interact.

Among the techniques that are used to obtain personal information are queries through the Internet. Only a few Internet users will send money to the deposed politician in Nigeria who will split his secret $15 million bank account with you for a token amount of operating money. There are, however, still very attractive offers on the Internet that tempt people to provide personal information. As more and more people have become familiar with these scams, they are refusing to take the bait. Moreover, many individuals and organizations are refusing to accept any email attachment because such attachments may be designed to support computer invasion.

Technology aids

In general, communications and computer technologies designed to gather personal information have progressed more rapidly and dramatically than those designed to protect this information. Serious efforts are being expended, however, to develop protection technologies.

One approach individuals can use to protect their private information is the Platform for Privacy Preferences Project (P3P). This protocol allows users to define the personal information they will allow to be seen by visited sites. When the user visits a site, P3P compares the requested information with the policies set by the user. If there are differences, P3P notifies the user and asks if he or she is willing to give the additional information requested. If not, P3P queries the site to see if this information is really required.

Another approach for achieving secure messaging is the use of Public Key Cryptography (PKC). The use of codes to protect the confidentiality of messages goes back thousands of years. Until fairly recently, however, even the most sophisticated codes required both message sender and message receiver to have the same key, i.e., a symmetric key. Keeping such keys updated and secure has always presented a major challenge. To address this problem, in 1976, Whitfield Diffie and Martin Hellman introduced the Public Key Cryptography (PKC) concept. In this concept, two keys are utilized — a public key that is open to anyone who wishes to use it and a private key known only to the person receiving the message.

Based on complex mathematic algorithms, this concept allows a person to encode a message using the receiver's public key. This coded message can be sent to the receiver over the Internet, but can be read only by the receiver using his or her own private key. Although the cost and effort required to employ PKC has limited its utilization, a number of factors have renewed interest in PKC, and there are strong indications that its use will grow in the future.

Group actions

Although there are actions that people can take individually to protect their own privacy, in many cases the only practical method to achieve this end is group action, particularly when governments are involved. These actions can include involvement in the political process, organized consumer protests, or protests by unorganized groups of dissatisfied users.

The federal government of the United States has adopted only limited formal legislation to protect privacy compared to Canada and most European countries. The Privacy Act of 1974 laid out restrictions on how the government itself may utilize private information it gathers on its citizens. The Computer Matching and Privacy Protection Act of 1988 extended the 1974 restrictions to take into account advances in computer technologies. There is legislation currently being considered by the U.S. Congress to protect citizens' health records. Given plans to automate such records, this legislation is of great importance.

In practice, the government's role in privacy protection is, for the most part, defined by the nation's courts or regulatory agencies, often as the result of actions by private issues groups. For example, the Electronic Privacy Information Center (EPIC) has recently petitioned the Federal Trade Commission (FTC) to investigate privacy protection policies related to the increasing use of "cloud computing" by organizations such as Google.

In similar manner, the World Privacy Forum (WPF) has petitioned the FTC to establish an anti-tracking measure, similar to the "Do Not Call List," that would allow users to block on-line advertisers from recording their Internet browsing habits for marketing purposes. In response to petitions of this type, Yahoo has committed itself to making its logs anonymous after 13 months, and Google and Microsoft will do the same after 18 months.

Although privacy groups are often at the center of public protest, there are examples of the impact of individuals acting on their own. This was demonstrated recently when Facebook decided to end its policy of using comments by users to advertise products on its network because of objections by individuals.

These and similar examples indicate that the public can take steps to protect privacy and that it is showing an increasing willingness to utilize this power.

Business opportunities

Given the advances in both hardware and software technologies, the premise that it is all but impossible for individuals and organizations to completely protect their privacy is probably valid. Therefore, the business opportunities offered in the privacy area are primarily those that increase the effort and costs involved in such compromise high enough to make privacy invasion unattractive and unprofitable, rather than those that eliminate the possibility of privacy compromise altogether. In searching for business opportunities, you should consider each of the techniques for countering invasions of privacy discussed above, i.e., personal caution, technology aids, and group action.

The primary source of privacy compromise is the failure of individuals to take the steps necessary to protect privacy. This failure is normally due to a lack of knowledge, lack of motivation, or excessive inconvenience in applying adequate safeguards. Therefore, training individual and groups in privacy protection measures presents business opportunities for small or medium-size companies. Such training could be provided by a number of methods, including seminars, personal conferences, instruction manuals, or "webinars." Consulting opportunities will also be available in areas such as analyzing existing privacy programs and recommending modifications as appropriate.

Business opportunities may also be afforded in the area of developing and initiating tools and techniques that make the application of appropriate procedures less burdensome and less expensive. A great deal of effort has already been expended in this area, and the development of new approaches will require imagination and ingenuity. Individuals either working alone or in companies of all sizes can demonstrate these traits.

In the continuing battle with those who seek to compromise private information, there are large potential business opportunities in the development of technologies that deter such compromise. The development, validation, and marketing of such techniques, however, are costly and complex activities, typically coordinated with professional groups such as the World Wide Web Consortium (W3C). Therefore, only companies with large resources and patient capital will normally be in a position to exploit such technologies.

In the area of group action, I see few business opportunities for either individuals or companies. The groups promoting changes in either the commercial or government arenas tend to be special interest groups with large numbers of volunteers and limited financial resources. Working with such groups and keeping aware of their activities, however, may provide ancillary benefits.

The recovery of private information from various repositories may prove particularly profitable. The current willingness of individuals to make their pictures, opinions, activities, group involvements, and other personal details widely available may prove troublesome in future job applications, requests for loans, political ambitions, and other desired activities. Many individuals will come to regret their earlier openness. There will be considerable demand for processes that can remove such information from the myriad of databases in which this information may be recorded.

Related to this, those offering reputation management services, i.e., tracking an entity's actions, other entities' opinions of those actions, and helping the entity manage the results, will be in great demand.

Discovery process: *In the process of conducting a series of technology forecasts for several government intelligence groups, I became increasingly aware of potential threats to classified information offered by advances in various related technologies and of techniques that could be used to counter these threats. It was evident that the general public was faced with similar threats, but that most people were not familiar with techniques for addressing these threats to personal privacy. I also found, however, that there was increasing public concern about privacy, and that various individuals and public policy groups were becoming more actively engaged in taking steps to protect their privacy.*

NEW APPROACHES IN GIVING AND RECEIVING ADVICE

Background

In making important decisions—personal, financial, business, etc.—it is common for individuals and organizations to seek expert advice. In larger companies, much of this advice comes from internal sources. These companies, however, will often utilize outside advisors. These advisers may represent large consulting firms, small or medium-size firms, or individuals. Generally, large firms are employed for strategic decisions, small and medium-size firms are employed for tactical decisions, and individuals are employed for narrowly focused advice. Consultants can be engaged on either a project or a continuing support basis.

> I often tell people to whom I am offering unsolicited advice that there are two good things about advice. First, you don't have to take it if you don't want to, and, second, such advice is usually free. Since I have been a hired consultant for more than three decades, I don't normally emphasize the second of these ideas! The reality, however, is the better the advice and the more adroitly it is offered, the more likely it will be accepted and acted on—and the better the outcome will be.

Large consulting firms, such as McKinsey & Company, the Boston Consulting Group, and Bain & Company, have large, multidisciplinary staffs, well-structured processes and procedures, huge computer capabilities, and long-standing reputations. When engaged for a specific project, a senior executive commonly takes part in the marketing and planning stages. Later, the actual analysis is conducted by a more junior employee who often is stationed with the client for the term of the contract. Typically, the client is charged on an hourly basis.

There are a very large number of small and medium-sized consulting firms, and they vary drastically in size, capabilities, procedures, and costs. Many of these firms specialize in specific technologies, products areas, geographical locations, and markets. Individual consultants, often university professors, bring special knowledge and experience that are focused on limited areas.

Current trends

Because of the ever-increasing power and ubiquity of information gathering, processing, and communicating technologies, the processes for seeking advice, for formulating and providing advice, and for assessing and acting on advice are undergoing fundamental changes. In the future, advice will:

- Be based on better information: Current and developing databases and search engines, both internal and external, will permit more efficient gathering, evaluating, and classifying of information.

- Be essentially real-time: Increased capabilities of computers and software will allow rapid modification of advice as situations change or more up-to-date information becomes available.

- Be based on wider input: Increased information technologies will permit input from large numbers of interested parties and the correlation of different ideas.

- Be shared more widely: The value of the offered advice to many people beyond those who specifically requested it will become increasingly well-recognized.

- Be better tailored to recipients: Having a basic understanding of the beliefs, lifestyles, and personalities of the people to whom the advice is offered will be increasingly useful to those providing the advice. Modern computer programs make this practical.

- Be tested against differing assumptions: Many organizations have found it useful to test decisions against a number of different assumption sets, e.g., alternate scenarios. Time and effort restrictions, however, have often limited the number of different scenarios that can be tested, as well as the number of factors that can be considered. With new computer capabilities, testing of many scenarios with many different factors is becoming feasible. (In Chapter Eight, I present more about the development and employment of alternate scenarios.)

- Be presented in more user-friendly formats: Language, written or oral, is typically the primary means of communicating advice. Many thoughts are difficult to communicate verbally, but presenting the advice in more perceptible formats such as YouTube-type videos, interactive computer games, or physical models will be much more practical than in the past.

- Often be offered without request: Improved computer programs will be increasingly capable of determining where unrequested advice will be useful to a recipient. For example, when one now reviews or orders a book on Amazon.com, other books based on previous reviews or orders are offered.

Business opportunities

To be successful in the future, advice providers, e.g., consultants, will have to be able to provide "up-to-the minute" advice to decision makers and convince decision makers of the special value of this "real time" advice.

New approaches to advice development, presentation, and utilization is resulting in a new landscape for the advice industry. This new landscape will open up new and expanded opportunities for individual consultants and smaller consulting firms. Traditionally, the larger consulting firms had a number of advantages over smaller firms:

- Greater access to information
- Access to a wider range of experts
- Greater resources such as personnel, computers, and funds
- Established client relationships

Although these advantages remain important, in the emerging advice environment they are becoming less important as computers, search engines, social networking platforms, and communications systems become increasingly powerful, versatile, and less costly. Moreover, the advantages of large consulting firms are now being matched by related disadvantages:

- Higher overhead costs
- Hierarchal, hard-to-change structures
- Standardized processes and procedures

Individual consultants and small consulting firms typically have more flexibility, can move more quickly, can better tailor advice to the needs of decision makers, and can often form more intimate relationships with clients than their larger cousins. In the future, successful consultants will have to be up-to-the-minute with the information they use to formulate their advice and be more closely involved with their clients.

Consultants must be both reactive to changing situations and proactive in projecting future trends and developments. The ability to determine what advice a client needs as opposed to what he or she may request provides a consultant with a significant competitive advantage over those without that ability. Because of these realities, small and medium-size firms will have increasing opportunities to expand their consulting businesses. (The difficulties currently being faced by the larger consulting firms are evidenced by the change in many firms' billing systems from hourly charges to fixed fees and outcome-based charges.)

Up to this point, I have targeted my comments to those individuals and organizations that provide external advice to users and have not addressed the provision of advice to decision makers within the organization. In general terms, however, the ideas presented also apply to individuals and groups within organizations. The recognition of the changing nature of advice and the ability to supply insightful advice to internal decision makers will always be a valuable asset for the professional advancement of individuals.

> An interesting vignette of the power of special knowledge is presented in the August/September 2000 issue of *Civilization*. In 1905, Mrs. Andrew Carnegie engaged a famous French milliner to design a special hat for Easter. After studying Mrs. Carnegie's face and body, the milliner selected a plain straw hat and pulled out a bright crimson ribbon. He carefully intertwined the ribbon in the hat, finishing the effect with an elegantly tied bow. Finally, he positioned the hat on Mrs. Carnegie's head at a particularly attractive angle. When the task was finished, Mrs. Carnegie looked at the creation in the mirror and proclaimed the result perfect. "How much do I owe you?" she asked. "Five hundred dollars" was the reply. "Five hundred dollars for a ribbon!" (Remember these were 1905 dollars.) "Mais, non, madam." the milliner replied with a smile as he removed the ribbon from the hat and placed it on her arm. "The ribbon is free." It was the flair and discernment of the milliner that gave such value to the inexpensive ribbon and the plain straw hat.

Discovery: I first became interested in the changing nature of advice by a short article in The New York Times. I then checked into the subject on Google. Among a number of related articles, I noted that the Conference Board had recently conducted a study on the area and had produced a series of articles on the subject by Michael Schrage, a Research Fellow at the MIT Sloan School's Center for Digital Business. Many of the ideas presented in this section were suggested by these articles.

EVOLUTION OF MEANINGFUL MATURITY

Background

The concept of a defined retirement age is a fairly new phenomenon. For most of history, people worked for as long as they were able and then depended on either their tribes or their families for whatever assistance they could provide. In Europe in the Middle Ages, trade guilds, fraternal societies, and formal groups of friends provided some assistance to their aging members. However, in 1883 Chancellor Otto von Bismarck initiated a government old-age program that was to serve as a model for many other countries.

Under this program, supported by funds provided by the government, employers, and the employees themselves during their working years, workers would receive a regular stipend on reaching the age of 70. Since the average life span in Germany at that time was 45 years, this was not a particularly large drain on the government. In 1916, after Bismarck had been dead for 18 years, the retirement age was reduced to 65 years. When a number of other counties adopted similar laws, the age of 65 became sort of a *de facto* definition of the retirement age.

In the United States, establishment of a formal retirement program did not take place until the Great Depression of the 1930s. As unemployment percentages reached the mid-20s, incentives grew to encourage older workers to leave the workplace. In 1935, the U.S. Congress passed, and President Franklin Roosevelt signed, the Social Security Act. In addition to several provisions for general welfare, the new Act created a social insurance program designed to pay retired workers 65 years old or older a continuing income after retirement.

A spokesman for the Committee on Economic Security explained that the premiums would start at one cent for each dollar earned up to $3,000 to be paid by the worker and an equal amount to be paid by the employer. These premiums would be raised by one-half cent every year until 1939, at which time the total premium for each worker and the employer would top out at three cents per dollar earned. The Committee stated that this would be "the most that anyone would ever pay."

In 1961, the age at which people would first be eligible for old-age insurance was lowered to 62, with benefits actuarially reduced. However, a 1983 law raised the age at which retirees could receive full benefits gradually from 65 to 67. Recently, the American Academy of Actuaries recommended that the full-benefit age be raised another two years to 69. Currently, almost 51 million retirees are receiving Social Security benefits.

Because the full benefit Social Security retirement age had been set in 1935 at 65 years, this became the age generally viewed as the proper one for workers to leave the workforce.

However, because many organizations based their retirement age on a combination of age and years of service, a large number of workers become eligible for retirement at an earlier age.

For example, U.S. Civil Service employees can generally retire at age 55 with 30 years service and, for certain special groups such as air traffic controllers, law enforcement, and firefighter personnel, the minimum retirement age is 50 with 20 years service. Members of the armed services can retire at half pay at the end of twenty years service and at three-quarters pay at the end of thirty years. Thus, a person who entered service at 18 could retire at half pay at 38 and three-quarters pay at 48.

At the same time that retirement age was decreasing for many workers, the average life expectancy was increasing from 69.0 in 1960 to 77.8 in 2005. On average, at the age of 65 years, a person can expect to live 18.7 more years; a 75-year-old person can expect to live another 12.0 years; and an 80-year-old person another 9.1 years.

Raymond Kurzweil, who was introduced in Chapter Three as a renowned futurist, has predicted that, in time, advances in health and medical technologies will allow people to live forever. To this end, he has engaged in a very disciplined life-style that he hopes will keep him alive until the necessary advances have been achieved. In case this doesn't work as he hopes, he has arranged to have his body frozen until technology will support restoration. In a related area, *The Lancet,* the world's largest medical journal, recently projected that most children born this century in advanced nations would live to be a least 100 years old.

Today's older citizens are in increasingly good physical and mental health because of medical advances in the treatment of diseases typically associated with old age, such as cancer, stroke, and heart disease, together with the passage of Medicare legislation in 1965 and Medicare Pharmaceuticals legislation in 2006. At the same time, these citizens tend to be considerably better educated and in better economic situations than similar age cohorts in the past. Because of these factors, in the late twentieth century, many individuals and couples were able to devote years, and even decades, to travel, sports, hobbies, charity work, movies, television, and other time diversions.

> A recent stylebook for news media professionals produced by the International Longevity Center in New York City and Aging Services in California indicated that referring to people beyond a certain age as "older people" or simply "man" or "woman" followed by their age, if their age is relevant to the story, is currently considered proper.
>
> Terms to be avoided include "elderly," "senior citizens," and the "golden years," and even terms such as "feisty," "spry," "grandmotherly," and "80 years young" are frowned upon. Absolutely forbidden are "biddy," "codger," "fogy," "fossil," and "geezer."

Current trends

Over the last couple of decades, many retired people have been quite satisfied with relatively sedentary lives. More recently, a number of people with Type A personalities (aggressive, competitive, impatient, time-conscious) and some with Type B personalities (more patient, relaxed, and easy-going) have begun to believe that there is more to later life than low golf scores, bridge master points, twelve hours of TV a day, and voyages on the Royal Caribbean. These individuals often seek more responsible positions in charitable, civic, political, or special cause organizations—or even return to the workplace.

A growing number of aging workers are either working longer before retirement or returning to the workplace. The U.S. Bureau of Labor Statistics estimates that 29% of those in their late 60s were still employed in 2006, up from 18% in 1985. Moreover, 27% of workers aged 45 and above indicated that they planned to continue to work past their voluntary retirement ages. Of those aged 55-64, 32% said they are pushing back their retirement plans. In the academic community in 2005, over 54% of full-time faculty members in the U.S. were over 50, compared to 22.5% in 1969.

Along with the desire to maintain the social and intellectual interactions associated with the workplace and the desire to have meaningful lives, economic factors are motivating many individuals to either remain in, or return to, the workforce. A commonly used rule-of-thumb for maintaining a livable income for the retirement years is to withdraw no more than four percent of one's investments each year. With recent decreases in stock, bond, real estate, and other investment prices, however, larger withdrawals are often necessary to maintain a given lifestyle.

At the same time that many older workers are interested in remaining in or returning to the workforce, a number of companies have become increasingly appreciative of the experience, loyalty, and diligent work habits of their older workers. Because of these factors it is almost certain that more and more individuals will remain active in the workforce on either a full-time or a part-time basis. The challenge will be to determine how to best utilize the experience, skills, and abilities of these people in a truly meaningful way.

Business Opportunities

The trend toward utilizing the experience and talents of older citizens more effectively will provide new opportunities for small and medium-size organizations. The effective employment of these citizens depends on the three factors—experience, skills, and abilities. These factors are interrelated, and attractive business opportunities will fall to those who can correlate them effectively.

Many of the individuals involved will prefer to continue in their current jobs or similar jobs, while many others will prefer—or be forced by company policy— to enter new fields. However, these individuals may not know how to transfer their skills and abilities to new fields and may be uncertain about their ability to contribute in a new undertaking. There will, therefore, be a need for businesses that can assist individuals in redefining their ambitions and their goals. Where attractive pathways can be defined, older workers will be motivated to remain in, or return to, the workforce in some capacity.

In the normal course of aging, individuals suffer decreases in stamina, physical abilities, and mental alertness. However, as opposed to physical capabilities, intellectual capabilities appreciate with use. Intellectual assets serve as a foundation for innovation, inspiration, problem resolution, and value creation. Of course, the abilities of older workers vary greatly depending on such factors as previous education and experience, general health, and intellectual involvement. Although there is some correlation between age and decreases in capabilities, the fact is that people's chronological age may be quite different from their functional age. Thus, there will be opportunities for small and medium-size businesses that can evaluate the capabilities—physical, mental, and emotional—of those interested in continuing in, or returning to, the workforce.

Once the capabilities of individuals are defined, the next step will be to identify specific opportunities that match these capabilities. Again, small and medium-size organizations that can assist in identifying these opportunities and in matching ability and need will provide valuable services. In many respects, this process is similar to those used by general employment agencies. Properly serving these market needs will require a different mindset, a different skill set, and a different business model. New approaches in training and education must be developed for older people. These challenges will leave an open door to enterprising companies and, in some cases, individuals

Another service to older people may prove especially lucrative. A growing body of evidence suggests that "mind training" can enhance the mental agility of older people, adding years to an individual's employment effectiveness. Individuals and groups that develop and conduct such training will attract a large audience of older people. Other attractive business opportunities include activities that reduce the difficulties of older workers such as providing easy transportation, new machinery that will simplify routine tasks, and administrative procedures that will make job-sharing more practical.

Although it is unlikely the provision of the described services on a commercial basis will be very attractive to large companies, these companies may be able to use such services to their own operational advantage. Many large companies have invested considerable time and effort in "knowledge management." This concept is based on the premise that the more senior workers have developed skills, insights, and "know how" that are not easily described but are of significant value to the organization.

Knowledge management involves specific processes for transforming this "implicit (indefinable) knowledge" into "explicit (definable) knowledge" that can be transferred to younger workers. An argument can be made that, since this implicit knowledge is so valuable, companies will do well to keep senior workers on the job longer so they can employ the accumulated knowledge directly. To do this, however, the company may have to conduct assessments and processes similar to the ones discussed above.

Discovery process: I first became interested in the area of meaningful maturity when my company, TFI, was engaged by a federal agency to conduct a study on Knowledge Management. In the conduct of this project, I was struck by the importance that many companies place on transferring the implicit knowledge of senior employees to younger employees. My interest was furthered by my participation in the Seminars for Adult Growth and Enrichment (SAGE) program conducted by the University of Texas at Austin, where I noted the number of men and women, well into their sixties, seventies and beyond, who were interesting, mentally alert, and, for the most part, physically fit. The effective utilization of the experience and talent of this group will materially enrich our society.

ALL VERY INTERESTING, BUT FRANKLY, SO WHAT?

Individuals seeking to take advantage of emerging Minitrends have considerable freedom in selecting the one(s) to exploit and in how to conduct that exploitation. Individuals in small and medium-size companies, on the other hand, have much less freedom in this regard; the selection of Minitrends and exploitation approaches must be done within an organization that already has structure, established processes and procedures, customer bases, company culture and customs, and conflicting priorities.

Typically, when a small or medium-size company undertakes to exploit a Minitrend, it does not abandon its basic business. For example, as I discuss in Chapter One, American Superconductor did not drop its other superconducting product lines when it moved into the wind power business, and, as my company, Technology Futures, Inc., entered new business areas, we continued to seek contracts in the areas in which we had developed expertise and established client bases.

A bad choice of either the Minitrend to be exploited or the way the in which that exploitation is to be conducted can result in serious financial and other problems for the company. Therefore, the decision to engage in Minitrend exploitation typically rests with the managers and executives, or at least the primary decision-makers. However, ideally, everyone in the organization should be involved in search for promising Minitrends and in performing early analyses. Although the attention of individuals and large companies to emerging Minitrends is important, for small and middle-size companies, such attention is essential.

If you are a manager or executive in a small or medium-size company you should not only search for promising Minitrends yourself, but you should also establish a culture that encourages employees at all levels to be alert for interesting Minitrends and to bring these trends to your attention when they appear promising.

If you are not in a management position, you should be on continuous alert for Minitrends that would be valuable to the company and, when appropriate, bring them to the attention of company management. When you do this you must first do your homework and be prepared to discuss your recommendation in a knowledgeable and well-considered manner.

Chapter Six

Minitrends for
Large Companies

As indicated in previous chapters, there are an almost infinite number of Minitrends that may be attractive to individuals or to small and medium-size companies. Some Minitrends, however, are more suitable for large companies because of the time and effort required to exploit them effectively. Such companies have the resources needed for development of a Minitrend, and, perhaps more important, they have the capability to fully benefit from the Minitrend if it proves profitable.

The commitment to develop a Minitrend by a large company involves diversion of funds, management attention, and support resources from current operations. Therefore, for a large company to commit to the development of a Minitrend, it must offer the promise of significant, long-term advantages.

The Minitrends that are appropriate for large companies may have many characteristics of Megatrends. The key factor that separates Minitrends is that most companies don't appreciate the potential significance of the trend, even though they may be aware of it.

In this chapter, I discuss three Minitrends that I believe could be of considerable importance to a number of large companies. However, as I discuss in each Business Opportunities section, there may also be attractive opportunities for individuals and small and medium-size companies.

ADVANCES IN DIGITAL MANUFACTURING

Background

Advanced digital manufacturing (ADM) encompasses a number of manufacturing technologies developed to reduce the design and production cycles of manufactured goods. In contrast to traditional machining processes that cut, bend, and machine a part from stock material, ADM utilizes layered manufacturing technologies that build parts from the addition of successive layers of material.

Using ADM, parts of an arbitrary shape can be created without the use of traditional machining processes. These traditional processes are often labor-intensive and involve a number of different steps and cutting tools. Although layered techniques typically do not produce parts as rapidly as traditional mass manufacturing processes, they eliminate the need for expensive machine tooling and setup procedures. As a result, complex, custom-made parts with arbitrary dimensions and features can be produced for prototyping and small production runs very quickly and at a much lower cost.

Essentially, every ADM system consists of two parts: (1) a computer-aided design (CAD) system and (2) a layered manufacturing machine that is capable of producing a part in successive layers according to instructions from the CAD system. In an ADM process, a designer first creates a three-dimensional representation of a part using CAD software such as AutoCad, ProEngineer, Inventor, or SolidWorks. The ADM software converts the program files into machine files that the operation machine can use to fabricate each layer of the part until it is complete. The final step of the process involves post-fabrication finishing and cleaning. This includes the removal of fabrication support materials and polishing and painting to improve the final appearance of the part (see Exhibit 6.1).

Exhibit 6.1. A Rapid Manufacturing Machine

Source: Phoenix Analysis and Design Technologies

There are a number of ADM fabrication techniques. Each uses some form of layered manufacturing methodology.

- **Stereolithography (SL),** the first commercial layer manufacturing system, creates parts using ultraviolet (UV) lasers and a photosensitive, UV curable polymer resin. The UV lasers traverse the path in the pattern dictated by the computer-generated files, causing the polymer resin to cure into the shape of a layer of the part. The part can then generate polymer prototypes, plastic molds for injection molding, or blocks for metal sheet forming.

- **Selective laser sintering (SLS)** enables the use of a broader range of materials than SL, including powders of metal, metal oxide, ceramic, plastic, and sand powders. These powders are deposited on a platform and a carbon dioxide (CO_2) laser is used to selectively sinter (melt) the powder into the CAD-generated shape for each layer. The yield strength and packing density of the final sintered part can be controlled by adjusting the scanning speed and power of the CO_2 laser (see Exhibit 6.2).

Exhibit 6.2. Selective Laser Sintering

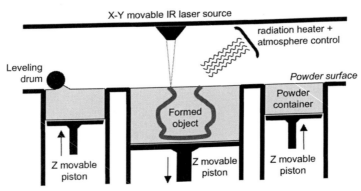

Source: Materialize

- **Shape deposition manufacturing (SDM)** combines layered manufacturing and traditional computer numerically controlled (CNC) machining. In SDM processes, each layer is machined (milled) after being created, and support material is added and machined to support subsequent layers. The use of the machining steps creates smoother surfaces in the final part and allows for layers with overhanging, undercut, and separated features to be supported during the layered fabrication process. SDM is typically used for custom tooling and precision assemblies and allows a high-quality surface finish, complex undercut features, and multi-material parts with inserts.

- **3D printing** uses inkjet printing technology to build 3D models in successive layers using ceramic, metal, and thermoplastic powders. In this process, powder is distributed on a "build platform." An inkjet print head moves across the powder selectively depositing liquid binder in the pattern dictated by the CAD files. The liquid binder creates a layer of bound powders into the shape of the desired layer. The unbound powder functions as a support for overhangs and undercuts. After the print heads have followed their dictated pattern for a particular layer, the part is lowered, more powder is added, and the process is repeated. When the part is complete, it can be fully sintered (fired) to reduce its porosity. (See Exhibit 6.3)

Exhibit 6.3. 3D Printing Process

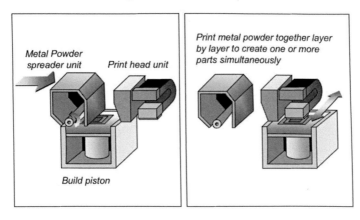

Source: ExtrudeHone

- **Bioplotting** is very similar to 3D printing except that it uses biomaterials for applications related to tissue engineering and drug delivery systems.

- **Layer object modeling (LOM)** bonds sheet material together in layers to form a laminated structure. Materials available to designers using this process include paper, plastic, water-repellent paper, ceramic, and metal powder tapes. Casting dies for automotive parts have used LOM for production.

The skills required for application of ADM processes fall into two broad categories: design and machine operations. The design technicians and machine operators work together closely to ensure that the final products of the ADM process are produced as accurately and inexpensively as possible.

Design technicians must possess a thorough understanding of advanced 3D modeling and simulation software and understand the conversion of design files into the machine format. They must also be able to troubleshoot these converted files and remove excess clutter that may result in unnecessary machine steps. These technicians must also have an understanding of the materials used in ADM processes and their suitability for different applications. Combining these skill sets, and using their knowledge of the capabilities of ADM processes, design technicians can compare and evaluate all available data on tolerances, function, manufacturability, cost, and expected quality. This assists them in making informed decisions about the creation of a 3D model for ADM fabrication.

ADM machine operators, on the other hand, must be familiar with the maintenance and management of ADM equipment. They must also have a basic familiarity with common shop equipment and machinery. In addition, model-making (finishing) skills such as polishing and sanding are a requisite. They are responsible for supplying appropriate build materials to the ADM machine and monitoring the process for irregularities during the build process.

For effective ADM applications, design technicians and machine operators must work hand-in-hand.

Current trends

A much more varied range of shapes, including intricate geometries and cavities, can be created quickly and efficiently since ADM designers are not constrained by the limitations of traditional machining and forming techniques—milling, drilling, lathe work, etc. ADM techniques are currently being used by a number of companies in a wide range of industries to reduce the amount of time and money required to introduce products to the market. As a result, ADM is becoming increasingly important in product development and manufacturing environments.

A number of companies in various industries are currently utilizing specific ADM technologies.

These include:

- **Automotive:** All major automakers use ADM to generate functional and non-functional (ornamental) prototypes in their research and development departments. Additionally, NASCAR and Formula One teams use

ADM to quickly build prototypes for aerodynamic performance testing and in some cases, custom made parts for the actual competition cars.

- **Aerospace:** Major aerospace manufacturers such as Boeing and Lockheed use ADM to manufacture low-volume, flight-ready components. The use of ADM avoids the cost and delay of developing expensive custom tooling for small production runs.

- **Military:** The Army is utilizing ADM to expedite the replacement of parts in battlefield operations (tank parts, etc). Additionally, the Navy is using ADM in fleet service.

- **Consumer goods:** The R&D departments of consumer goods manufacturers often use ADM to produce relatively small production runs of new products. These produced goods can be used to conduct market surveys that allow manufacturers to assess the "marketability" of a product before committing to a full-blown production and marketing campaign.

- **Biomedical:** This is a rapidly growing area of ADM application. Using ADM, laboratories are able to convert MRI and CT images into models of a patient's joints and bones. Surgeons can use these models to test surgical procedures before an actual operation. Additionally, hearing aid manufacturers use ADM to produce custom-fitted, in-the-ear devices.

Over the years, a number of ADM techniques capable of using a greater variety of materials have been developed. These material advances have increased the size and durability of produced parts, and ADM vendors have increased the quality and repeatability of their machines. As a result, ADM is frequently used not only to fabricate functional prototypes, but also for small production runs of custom designed parts.

There are a number of factors that are driving the increasing use of ADM. These include:

- **Improvements in the yield rates of ADM machines:** These improvements have allowed manufacturers to fabricate series production parts in quantities of one to several thousand. This has expanded the market for ADM machines among custom manufacturers.

- **Time-to-market considerations:** Product manufacturers are always under pressure to reduce product design and manufacturing cycles (time-to-market). ADM tools reduce the number of steps in the engineering and manufacturing process, enabling users to improve their performance in this area.

- **Advances in 3D CAD modeling and simulation software:** Solid design and simulation software packages that allow engineers to design and test the performance of parts before a prototype is built are becoming more powerful and less expensive. The designs generated by these packages can be easily converted into formats usable by ADM machines. As more manufacturers adopt these packages and learn about the capabilities of ADM, the demand for ADM machines will rise.

- **Increasing variety of materials:** Technical advances have allowed for the use of a wider range of materials in ADM machines. This variety, which includes more durable materials, allows users to create an increasing number of parts that are actually functional and not just concept models. This expanded ability to create functional parts will allow manufacturers to test designs more quickly and less expensively, which is a major driver for their ADM purchases.

Business opportunities

The continuing advances in ADM technology offer significant advantages to a wide range of industries involved in various manufacturing processes. These advantages include improved products, more efficient production, improved yields, greater flexibility in materials and processes, and shorter time-to-market for new products.

The expense of installing and operating new ADM equipment is often quite high, and large output is required before reduced production costs justify this expense. (Typical purchase costs are in the low-to-mid six-figure range, with maintenance costs running about $30,000 per year. A number of 3D printing machines are available from anywhere from $40,000 to $70,000.)

Because of high cost involved, large companies are typically the ones that initiate major ADM installations equipment — and receive the benefits of this installation. Once the equipment is installed, there may be an attractive business in contracting its use to smaller companies. Most large manufacturing companies have probably already considered the applicability of ADM to their operations. However, they may not be completely aware of recent advances in the technology and the significant advantages offered by these advances.

The high cost/benefit ratio of purchasing and installing new ADM equipment may present a barrier to many small and medium-size companies. On the other hand, these companies may be able to overcome these barriers and take advantage of the special ADM capabilities by partnering with other similar size companies to share costs, leasing equipment from larger companies, contracting with larger companies for specific services, or purchasing less-sophisticated or used ADM equipment.

The range of skills required for proper application of ADM processes means that skilled individuals and small groups of individuals will be in demand as advisors, consultants, and trainers to companies using ADM on a one-time or a continuing basis. They may also organize themselves to produce limited runs of specialized items. For this purpose, they may contract with larger companies to use their ADM equipment.

Discovery Process: *Although I have been interested in automated manufacturing for some time, I was unaware of recent advances in ADM technology until I attended a conference on the subject being conducted at a nearby convention center. At this conference, a variety of ADM equipment was displayed, and a number of qualified experts discussed the current and projected state of the art.*

Attendance at this conference and the exhibition, together with discussions with presenters and other attendees, convinced me of the growing importance of this technology.

INCREASING USE OF ELECTRICITY IN INDUSTRIAL PROCESSES

Background

Electricity is a unique source of energy. Unlike a hot combustion gas, electricity is a "converted" energy form, i.e., it is 100% "available." This means that electrical energy can interact with matter in direct and highly controllable ways, in contrast with thermal energy, which is limited in the manner and extent of its ability to produce material transformations. Over the last few decades, significant industrial penetration by electrotechnologies has occurred. This penetration, however, has been limited primarily by economic factors.

Electricity has a number of characteristics that are particularly valuable in industrial processes. These include:

- **Simplified power distribution:** The simplification of power distribution associated with electrically based production systems is an asset in terms of process flexibility, reduced space and capital costs, and an improved working environment.

- **High power density:** Electromagnetic energy can be transferred to materials at very high power densities (a million times those of combustion sources). Increased power density translates directly into increased rate of production and usually results in increased efficiency of energy use and reduced emissions.

- **Media independence:** Electromagnetic energy does not require a transfer medium in contrast with fuel-driven processes that produce hot combustion gases and use those gases to transfer energy to the product. This independence permits processing in a vacuum, and also allows engineers to select process media that have desired characteristics. This capability eliminates the degrading effects produced by contact with combustion products, improves product quality, and allows production at lower temperatures. This can provide better energy and material utilization and reduce emissions.

- **Volumetric energy deposition:** Electricity has the unique capability to generate heat within a body of matter. In bypassing the gaseous layer that forms the primary resistance to heat transfer in a convectively heated product, this property allows much faster heating than conventional processes. This translates into smaller equipment and, thus, smaller process space. This is particularly important in processes demanding clean, uncluttered environments, such as semiconductor processing. In heating billets for steel forgings, heating time can be reduced by a factor of 50, yielding fourfold reductions in material loss due to oxidation.

- **Controllability-associated attributes**: The ability to exercise process control is particularly pertinent in the context of the Information Age, since control is literally the continuous acquisition and use of information in processing. The rapid rise of digital computing as an element of process control, coupled with the evolution of a host of new techniques for sensing process parameters, has created a new impetus for the use of basic process technologies with a high degree of controllability.

- **Focusability and spatial control:** Some forms of electromagnetic energy, e.g., lasers and electron beams, can be focused to a high degree of accuracy and positioned with great accuracy. The ability to focus energy permits temperatures capable of melting or vaporizing even high melting-point materials. For example, the extreme spatial resolution allows photolithography processes to lay down the circuit patterns etched into silicon wafers in integrated circuit production.

- **Directional control:** Electrical energy can be controlled in direction as well as intensity, allowing directional information to be easily imparted to the product. This can increase process flexibility and provide the designer with additional freedom in the configuration of materials.

- **Time response:** Pure electromagnetic wave energy sources are massless. Hence, they can respond to control inputs limited only by the rate at which the control fields themselves can be varied, typically a matter of milliseconds. Electron beams or lasers can be controlled at a rate comparable to the response time of electronic sensing elements. The highly-flexible electronically-based production control systems can respond to changing inputs at near-computer speeds. The precise control of energy flow reduces material and energy losses and allows tighter control of product specifications. By reducing waste, adverse environmental effects are also alleviated.

- **Electromagnetic selectivity:** Electromagnetic fields interact with matter through the electrical properties of the atoms and molecules themselves. This allows different energy deposition in different substances. For example, high-frequency electromagnetic waves can be used to excite water molecules in preference to other substances. Electrolysis, the separation of ionic species based on their electrical charge, is another example of electromagnetic selectivity. Electromagnetic selectivity permits production of high purity products with often superior properties.

Manufacturing can be defined as the transformation of materials from one form to another more valuable form using energy and information. In general, the greater the information content of the process, the greater the efficiency, the smaller the waste of material and energy, and the smaller the pollution-producing side streams will be. For example, sand can be used as filler for asphalt, as a component of fine china, or as an ingredient in an electronic computer chip. The basic difference between these uses is the amount of information embedded in the silicon (sand) during the production process. Electrical processes can be used to materially increase information content to material. These conceptual relationships are illustrated in the following diagram.

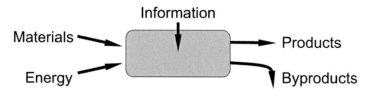

Source: Industrial Electrification in the Information Age
Edison Electric Institute

Current trends

Because of the listed characteristics, electric power has been used in industrial processes for decades. The use of electric power has been limited by the fact that enabling technology has not been available to take full advantage of its unique characteristics. The ability to modify energy deposition rates in a microsecond is of little value if it takes minutes to realize the need for modification. The ability to machine to micron-level precision is not particularly useful if one can only measure to millimeter accuracy. There are, however, a number of emerging factors that are motivating much greater use of electricity in various industrial processes.

- **Advances in control technologies**. Advances in microelectronics, computer controls, and information technologies are profoundly altering the way that goods are developed, produced, and distributed. These changes require the attributes of electrically-based processes that have no counterpart in traditional process technologies. This trend toward computer-centered process controls will reinforce the current wave of electric process penetration. In the industries of the future, the information element of manufacturing will increasingly define technology choices. Those companies best able to integrate information flow into their processes will ultimately win out over those who are less adaptable.

- **Changing customer needs**. Products evolve in response to changing consumer needs and technological capabilities. In the future:

  - Consumer products will possess increasing technical complexity or information content.
  - New products and services will facilitate greater convenience and automation in lifestyles.
  - New communications and information-related industries will continue to emerge.
  - Greater miniaturization will be achieved in many products.
  - There will be an expansion in product variety.

- **Increasing global competition**. Intensified global competition has significantly altered the market for many goods and services as markets are becoming more regional and global in nature. In this environment, the demand for increased diversity and quality of products, intense time-based competition, and close scrutiny of environmental impacts will cause companies to take a new look at technologies that offer maximum flexibility, efficiency, and environmental compatibility. For a variety of reasons, these technologies are, in most instances, electrically based.

- **Increasing concern about the environment.** In an era of heightened awareness and concern about the environment, the term "clean energy" has taken on new meaning and importance. Producing products in an environmentally responsible way has become not only desirable, but often critical to continued operation. In many instances, electrotechnologies will provide the most attractive option for achieving both environmental and economic objectives. Electrotechnology can contribute to more environmentally friendly processes in four ways:

- Reduction of byproducts and emissions from energy conversion: It is a common misconception that electrotechnologies are more primary-energy-intensive than fuel-based technologies because of the energy conversion loss at the power plant. In fact, in many instances the contrary is true when total energy expenditure is considered.

- Reduction of byproducts and emissions from process steps: Electricity-based processes have been shown to be particularly well-suited for waste minimization in various applications.

- Recovery and reuse of process by-products: Several electrotechnologies are moving into industrial use for the recovery of otherwise wasted and hazardous byproducts, including recovery of heavy metals from process residual dust, aluminum from smelting and casting dross, and hydrogen and sulfur from hydrogen sulfide in natural gas.

- Remediation of process emissions: Remediation of hazardous emissions from industrial operations to render them harmless or to restore contaminated areas is often a difficult problem with conventional thermal or chemical techniques. Electrotechnology-based solutions include a plasma process to vitrify soil contaminated with metal processing wastes and separation processes for removal of hazardous contaminants from both liquid and gaseous waste streams. Applications include selective removal of trace organics from chemical solutions and supercritical oxidation processes for the treatment of water containing particularly difficult contaminants.

Based on these factors, it appears very probable that the next few years will see continuing growth in the use of electricity in industrial processes.

Business Opportunities

Introducing electrotechnologies into industrial processes usually involves very large capital investments and will typically fall under the aegis of large companies. To remain competitive in an increasingly global market, such investments may well be necessary.Large companies should carefully consider the advantages and disadvantages of making such investments. Given current interest in environmental protection, the relative importance of different economic factors may be changing.

Although converting to electrotechnologies will typically be restricted to large companies, the conversions will normally involve the design, installation, and maintenance of a variety of information-based technologies such as lasers, e-beam systems, electronic controls, and new software and firmware. Individuals and small and medium-sized companies may be well suited to provide support in each of these areas.

Conversion to new electrical-based processes will result in major changes in business operations including pricing, marketing, human resource management, etc. Thus, there may be opportunities for individuals to serve as consultants in the planning and implementation of process conversions.

Discovery process: As a nuclear engineer I was always interested in the production, transmission, and distribution of electric power. I became especially involved with industrial electric power processes when I was invited by a former colleague at the University of Texas at Austin, Dr. Philip Schmidt, to join him, Dr. Frederick Sparrow of Purdue University, and Dr. Jay Zarnikau of Planergy, Inc., in the conduct of a study on the subject for the Edison Electric Institute.

NEW APPLICATIONS OF NANOTECHNOLOGY

Background

The term "nanotechnology" is commonly used to define substances in which at least one dimension is one hundred nanometers or less. (A nanometer [nm] is one billionth of a meter, a very short length. For comparison, a human hair is about 50,000 nm in diameter. A more picturesque analogy is that a nanometer is the length that a man's beard would grow in the time it takes for him to raise his razor from a sink top to his face.)

Because of their large surface to volume ratio and various quantum mechanics effects, nano-sized particles often have very different physical, electrical, chemical, and optical properties from the same substance at macro-size. These properties often provide very unique and useful characteristics to nanomaterials.

- Nano-sized iron particles can absorb great amounts of contaminants, such as lead and arsenic, from water. These particles can then be removed easily by magnetic methods.

- Nano-size aluminum particles can be a more powerful explosive than TNT.

- Nano-sized silver can act as a very potent disinfectant against a large spectrum of bacteria. Moreover, because of its electrical conductivity and its transparence to visible light, nano-sized silver can be used to create transparent conductive films for items such as PDAs and monitors.

- Silicon can be changed from an insulator to a semiconductor or even a conductor at nano-size, which makes it a very promising candidate for various electronic applications.

- Zinc oxide sunscreens, which are normally an unsightly white, become transparent when reduced to nano-size.

- Many vitamins that are insoluble in water become soluble when reduced to nanoparticle size.

Throughout the world, researchers in universities and commercial organizations are working to develop practical applications that utilize the unique properties of nanomaterials.

In January 2008, the University of Texas at Austin was chosen to manage a new Advanced Energy Consortium that will address ways in which nanotechnology techniques can be used to improve the production of oil, both in the United States and in other countries. The supporting companies, BP America, Inc., Baker Hughes, Inc., the Conoco-Philips Company, Halliburton Energy Services, Inc., Marathon Oil Corp., Occidental Oil and Gas, and Schlumberger, Ltd., will contribute a million dollars a year for three years to support the research. Rice University will be a collaborative technical partner. Potential applications include increases in the amount of oil recovered from individual wells and fields and better monitoring of fields by micro and nanosensors.

Carbon nanotubes represent a particularly interesting form of nanomaterials. These nanostructures are characterized by diameters in the nano range, but with lengths tens of millions of times longer. Carbon nanotubes are the strongest and stiffest material on earth in terms of tensile strength and elastic modulus (300 times as strong as high-carbon steel). These properties are already being utilized in some consumer goods, such as bicycles and tennis racquets, and promise to be of increasing importance in construction, aerospace, petroleum, and other industries as they become less expensive and more available in the future.

Examination of samples of Damascus Steel swords, known for centuries for their strength and ability to maintain sharpness, have shown that these characteristics are almost certainly due to carbon nanotubes formed during the production process. These nanotubes were apparently created during the forging process, which proves that there is more than one way of a achieving a desired end.

Carbon nanotubes also offer some very interesting electrical and heat transfer properties. For example, the electric characteristics of carbon nanotubes can be varied by their particular structure. In one structure, the nanotubes can act as semiconductors, and, in another structure, they can serve as excellent electric conductors (in theory, 1,000 times greater than copper or aluminum). These characteristics make them very promising in the microelectronic area.

Researchers at Florida State University have recently developed "buckypaper," a paper-thin composite of carbon nanotubes that promises to be 10 times lighter and 500 times stronger than steel sheets. The buckypaper has strong electric conductivity and heat dispersion characteristics and will be extremely useful in automobiles, aircraft, computers, television, and other products. FSU faculty members are currently working on techniques for manufacturing buckypaper economically and in quantity and are projecting commercial applications in the relatively near future.

Current trends

Because nanomaterials are currently being used in a number of commercial products, you may wonder why I classify the applications of nanotechnology as a Minitrend. My reason is my belief that the technology has reached a critical point where its employment in a number of fields is going to increase rapidly. Moreover, it appears that most individuals and organizations are either not aware of this situation or do not appreciate its significance.

One factor that has limited both scientific research and commercial applications of nanotechnologies has been the great difficulty and high cost of producing single-walled carbon nanotubes (SWNT). In 2000, the cost of producing a gram of SWNT was $1,500.

By 2007, this cost had been reduced to $50-100, and improved production approaches continue to both reduce cost and significantly increase output. These facts will have a snowballing effect as increased availability of SWNTs not only increases commercial appeal, but also supports the development of new applications.

Research in the use of nanotechnology is beginning to pay off. The growing promise of nanotechnology was reflected in an August 2009 estimate by the Project on Emerging Nanotechnologies (PEM) that there are more than 1,000 manufacturer-identified nanotech products currently available and that this number is growing by three to four per week. (At http://www.nanotechproject.org/, PEM lists current products by name, category, company, and country.) As nanotech research continues and experience grows, additional applications are constantly being developed in areas as diverse as medicine, energy, communications, consumer goods, and heavy industries.

Current applications include:

- **Unidym** is commercializing printable electronic materials based on carbon nanotubes. Unidym's focus is on the production of clear conductive films for touch panel displays and thin film solar cells. The transparent, conductive films are made with carbon nanotubes that are intended to replace transparent conductive films produced with Indium Tin Oxide, which has many shortcomings.

- **OxFrac** is developing spherical aluminum oxide particles that can be used to enhance the recovery rate and total recovery of natural gas from certain types of wells.

- **eXceed Filter** has developed and commercialized a nanofiber-based air filter media that can trap large quantities of dust and viruses. The filters have applications in hospitals, clean rooms, and data centers.

- **Magnano Technologies** is developing Iron Oxide nanoparticles that can be used as contrasting agents for MRIs of metastatic tumors, which cannot be detected with existing contrast agents.

- **Angstrom Medica, Inc**. has produced a nanoparticulate-based synthetic bone that can be used in areas where natural bone is damaged or removed, such as in the treatment of fractures and soft tissue injuries.

- **Kodak** is producing organic light emitting diode (OLED) color screens, made of nanostructured polymer films, for use in audio systems and cell phones. OLEDs may enable thinner, lighter, more flexible, less power consuming displays and other consumer products such as cameras, PDAs, laptops, televisions, and other as yet undreamed of applications.

- **Shenhua Group**, China's largest coal company, has licensed technology from Hydrocarbon Technologies that will enable it to liquefy coal and turn it into gas. The process uses a gel-based nanoscale catalyst, which improves its efficiency and reduces the cost.

- **Argonide Nanomaterialsan, Inc**. makes a filter composed of nano-size alumina fiber that is capable of filtering the smallest of particles. This disposable filter retains 99.9999+% of viruses at water flow rates several hundred times greater than virus-rated ultra porous membranes.

- **Abraxis BioScience, Inc.**, a biotechnology company dedicated to delivering progressive cancer therapeutics to patients and medical professionals, recently announced the launch of Abraxane. To form Abraxane, the pharmaceutical paclitaxel (Taxol) is attached to nano-sized albumin for the treatment of metastatic breast cancer. This treatment is less toxic than regular Taxol and more effective in treating the cancers.

In the medical field, nanotech research is also beginning to pay off in the areas of diagnostics, drug delivery, and disease treatment. In the diagnostic area, certain substances and activities can be detected more easily and more effectively when nanoparticles are attached. Because of the increased selectivity in identifying diseased cells that nanoparticles offers, treatments can be more selectively targeted, limiting collateral damage to healthy cells. In the drug delivery area, nanotech carriers can be used to enhance the effectiveness of a drug while reducing undesirable side effects.

A very interesting application of nanotechnology in the medical field is a treatment for cancer currently being developed commercially by BioSpectra.

This treatment is based on research developed jointly by Rice University and the M.D. Anderson Cancer Research Institute. When reduced to nano-size, the color of gold depends on the size of the particles, e.g., red, blue, or green. In this treatment process, gold particles of a size that corresponds to visible light are attached to biological molecules that migrate to the location of the cancer. The patient is then subjected to a beam of light of the matching color. The energy of the light is deposited in the gold particles, raising their temperature, and burning up the cancerous cells. Visible light can penetrate about fifteen centimeters (roughly six inches) into the body without damaging non-cancerous tissue, contrary to current radiation treatments.

One of the issues that has restricted the application of nanotechnologies has been concern about possible adverse implications of the widespread use of these technologies. Many people are concerned that the extremely small size of these particles may result in unexpected health and environmental problems, e.g., because of their small size, nanoparticles can enter the body through a multitude of routes and can easily find a path into cell membranes.

These are legitimate concerns, and a number of governmental bodies throughout the world are seeking to better define these problems and to craft laws and regulations to address them. The U.S. National Institute for Occupational Safety and Health is already offering interim guidelines for working with nanomaterials. Moreover, nanotechnology researchers and product developers are learning from the mistakes of the past and are seeking to assess the risk of using nanotechnology before product commercialization.

In 2003, Technology Futures, Inc. (TFI) conducted a technology forecast on nanotechnology for the Texas State Technical College System (TSTC). In this forecast, we projected that by 2008:

(1) electronic/information technologies, nanoelectromechanical systems, and drug delivery, design and development, would present "large commercial opportunities" for nanotechnologies

(2) diagnostics, screening, and tagging technologies would present "important commercial opportunities"

(3) tools and instruments, and nanomaterials, e.g., metal and ceramic nanopowders, fullerenes, and carbon nanotubes, would present "modest commercial opportunities"

Download this forecast, "Nanotechnologies: A Technology Forecast," at http://www.tfi.com/minitrends/nanotechnology.html.

Business opportunities

The special characteristics of nanomaterials and the increasing understanding of how these characteristics can be gainfully utilized virtually guarantees attractive business opportunities for both individuals and companies. In a recent issue, the *Scientific American* magazine predicted that, by 2015, products incorporating nanotech will contribute approximately $1 trillion to the global economy; about two million workers will be employed in nanotech industries; and three times that many will have supporting jobs.

The unfolding nature of nanotechnology possibilities was demonstrated at a recent *Nanotechnology Venture Forum* conducted by the Rice University Alliance for Technology at which various nanotech start-up companies presented business plans to five venture capital firms. The breadth of potential opportunities for such start-up companies was indicated by the fact that the products offered by these companies included items such as high temperature batteries, nanostructured steel wires, devices to control electric static discharge, human organ assistance devices, negative reflective index materials, tumor treatment, and textile enhancement.

As both the research and the business communities learn more about how nanotechnology can be effectively utilized, many new applications of the technology will evolve. Although these applications will provide interesting opportunities for individuals and companies of all sizes, many of the most significant applications will fall under the aegis of large companies. To date, the most prevalent use of nanotech in large companies has been in the use of bulk nanotech materials to improve the quality of selected products such as scratch-resistant finishes or stain-proof clothing. Many large companies, however, have either begun using nanotechnologies in new roles or are planning to do so.

Many of the most important applications for large companies will not be in new products as such, but in improved manufacturing processes. For example, the cost of producing integrated circuit wafers is skyrocketing. (It is estimated that the cost of a state-of-the-art wafer fab is approaching 5-10 billion dollars.) The special electrical characteristics of nano-materials, e.g., high conductivity, ability to serve as conductors, semiconductors or resisters, the ability to be digitally switched by a single electron, and very high frequency tube oscillation capability, may drastically simplify processes and lower costs. This, of course, doesn't suggest a "Mom-and-Pop" operation.

In similar manner, large medical organizations will have primary responsibility for the development of new uses for nanomaterials in medical applications. Likewise, major energy companies will play a lead role in the use of nanotechnologies in oil discovery and production, while aircraft and automobile manufacturers, giant construction companies, and top building material suppliers will utilize the special mechanical properties of nanotechnologies.

Although large businesses will be involved in many of the most important uses of nanotechnology, the special characteristics of nanomaterials will also offer interesting opportunities for small and medium-size businesses by opening up new product lines or by increasing the efficiency and effectiveness of current activities.

Overall, as both researchers and users gain experience in how to utilize the special characteristics of nanomaterials more effectively, important business opportunities will arise for alert individuals and their companies.

Discovery process: Although I had been interested in nano-technology for a number of years, my special involvement in the area came at the suggestion of Michael Bettersworth, Associate Vice Chairman for Technology Development for the Texas State Technical College System (TSTC). TFI was working with TSTC to identify emerging technologies that would offer attractive new employment opportunities for its students. Mr. Bettersworth suggested that we conduct a technology forecast on nanotechnology as part of this program. During this project, TFI member Henry Elliott and I interviewed a number of people involved in nanotech research and employment, which whetted our appetites for the subject.

ALL VERY INTERESTING, BUT, FRANKLY, SO WHAT?

As I indicate in the Preface, the objective of this book is "to materially improve your business situation, your financial standing, and your personal satisfaction." The objective is not necessarily to add to the profits of an IBM, Exxon, or Microsoft. The question is, how can you use Minitrends to achieve your own goals and objectives if you are an employee of a large company?

Your challenge is to identify and analyze Minitrends that could be of significant value to the company and to define the specific advantages and disadvantages of the Minitrend to the company. When you fully understand the nature of the Minitrend and have analyzed its potential importance, you should bring this to the attention of company management in a manner that provides a basis for decisions as to whether and how the Minitrend should be exploited. As I mention earlier, larger companies are often more interested in acquiring a company that has already demonstrated success in the application of the Minitrend than in initiating a new program in-house. You may, therefore, have to both analyze attractive Minitrends and also identify companies already involved in exploiting these opportunities.

As an employee of a large company you may have less latitude in exploiting an attractive Minitrend than an individual or even an employee of a small or medium-size company. However, being familiar with the principles of Minitrend exploitation and utilizing that familiarity to uncover and analyze a range of Minitrends, particularly ones that may be of importance to your company, will still be to your advantage.

If your recommendations are followed and the exploitation of the Minitrend proves successful, you will undoubtedly improve your status in the company. Even if your recommendations are not followed, you will still get credit for your initiative in uncovering a potential new product or service line.

Part IV: Prospering from Minitrends

The final step in profiting from gems is converting the individual stone into alluring jewelry. Similarly, to profit from a Minitrend, you must determine the ones that are most attractive, develop a plan for taking full advantage of them, and execute that plan effectively.

Chapter Seven

Selecting a Minitrend
for Exploitation

After you have identified a small number of promising Minitrends that you believe may provide attractive business opportunities, the next task is to decide which of the Minitrends you wish to exploit. The first step in this process is examining the overall attractiveness of the Minitrends you have identified for consideration. There are two factors to consider in this examination: (1) the Minitrends' attractiveness to the business community as a whole and (2) their attractiveness to you individually and to your particular circumstances.

In considering the relative attractiveness of the Minitrends, keep in mind the basic premises of Minitrends, i.e., that the trend is already emerging, that its importance is not widely recognized, that it promises to become significant in a reasonably short period of time (two to five years), and that the Minitrend will provide a special advantage to those who identify and appreciate its implications and importance.

EXAMINE THE OVERALL ATTRACTIVENESS OF THE MINITREND TO THE BUSINESS COMMUNITY

Define the exact nature of the Minitrend you intend to exploit

First, as indicated in previous chapters, you must identify the trends you wish to exploit in general terms. Reducing the scope of consideration is, however, necessary when examining the overall attractiveness of a particular Minitrend. In considering the exploitation of the "Virtual Life" Minitrend discussed in Chapter Four, for example, you might wish to concentrate on the virtual world as a trial for marketing and advertisement, as a test arena for new products and processes, or as a forum for communication. In considering the "Increased Interest in Privacy" Minitrend discussed in Chapter Five, you might concentrate on new methods for protecting against hackers, new techniques for recovering undesired information from databases, or the actions of anti-intrusion groups.

In general, individuals or small groups of individuals should keep the scope of their concentration rather narrow, while established organizations will normally scope their efforts more broadly.

Define the special attractiveness of the Minitrend

The basic premise of the successful application of a Minitrend is that it must offer a new approach to a product, process, or procedure, and it must have one or more of the following characteristics:

- Be capable of inciting enthusiasm among potential users

- Open up opportunities for the individuals and companies involved

- Have special features that differentiate it from current norms

The first step in evaluating the business opportunities afforded by the Minitrend is to clarify what is special about the Minitrend that will support its takeover of the markets to which it is applicable. These special features will be the key drivers for success.

Because of this reality, determining what the special advantages of the Minitrend will be is essential. These special advantages will depend, of course, on the market group to be targeted. This matching of markets and Minitrends must be done iteratively. That is, you should define the general attributes of the Minitrend and then consider market groups for which these attributes would be valuable. You can then examine more carefully how these market groups could best utilize the Minitrend's special attributes. Issues to be considered include:

- What would be the specific advantages of the Minitrend to these potential users?

- What problems will the Minitrend solve?

- What new capabilities will be provided?

- How are the needs of these users now being satisfied?

- How much improvement over present approaches does the new Minitrend offer?

- How can those improvements be demonstrated to potential users?

In examining the match between Minitrends and customers, we at Technology Futures find it very useful to employ the concept of "careabouts." The premise of this concept is that all customers have certain issues that are very important to them, but which, for various reasons, they do not express — or sometimes even realize. Thus, if you ask them what they want, they may not make their desires clear. We sometimes find that even when we provide clients with just the product or services they request, they are less than delighted. To overcome this situation, we typically work very hard to determine what our customers truly care most about and will be delighted with when we provide it.

This "careabout" approach is particularly important in exploiting Minitrends because they typically represent new ideas and approaches of which the clients are not aware, but with which they will be very pleased when they see the results. Nobody ever asked for a microwave oven or a Frappuccino or a website until they had seen one.

Analyze the size and nature of potential markets

An essential step in the analysis process is examining not only the nature of potential markets, but also the size of these markets. The larger the size of the potential market, the more attractive the pursuit of the Minitrend application will be. Consideration of ancillary markets that might develop in the future is also important. In examining the size of the potential market, you must realize that the overall size of the market is not what must be considered, but rather the size of the market for which the Minitrend will have special attraction. The size of an attractive market will be larger for an established company than for an individual or small group of individuals initiating a new business adventure.

In evaluating the attractiveness of a given Minitrend, you must consider not only the size and nature of the potential market, but also the dynamics of market development. When new ideas and approaches emerge, a large portion of the customer base will be reluctant to accept them. People understand the old ideas and approaches; they have alliances and contacts based on the old; their reputations are based on their understanding and familiarity of the old ideas and approaches; and this is where the real money appears to be. People see new ideas and approaches as potential threats to their status and well-being and are reluctant to accept and adopt emerging innovations.

In addition to the social impediments to the acceptance of new ideas and approaches, new approaches are almost always initially inferior to the old ones in terms of the typical measures of worth. The new approach must have some characteristic that is of particular value to one segment of the market for it to be successful. This segment is often small, but not particularly cost-sensitive. Adoption by this segment paves the way for continuing improvement in the approach, which can open up new market segments which are larger, but more cost sensitive. If the new approach is truly superior to the old, this process of approach improvement/market expansion will continue until the new approach has taken over the entire market for which it is suited.

When initially introduced, transistors were more expensive, less reliable, and had poorer reproductive characteristics than comparable vacuum tubes. However, their light weight, small size, and low power requirements made them particularly attractive to the hearing aid market in which cost was not a major factor. The use of transistors in hearing aids and other devices with similar requirements provided initial funding for further research and developments.

In a similar manner, early mainframe computers were huge, expensive, and limited in capability. However, they were of significant value to the military forces by providing a tool for developing artillery flight tables. Since costs were of only minor importance to a nation at war, the federal government provided funding for the development of these computers. This funding supported continuing developments in the technology.

The first commercial use of electric lighting was not in lower Manhattan as is generally believed, but rather aboard ships. The reduction in fire hazards provided by electric lights clearly motivated their use regardless of cost. This usage demonstrated the practicality of these lights and gave experience in their use.

Consider where the Minitrend is in the emergence process

Success in the exploitation of a Minitrend is greatly impacted by the timing of its initiation. If you attempt to launch a Minitrend-based project or program too early, you may suffer unacceptable disappointments and expenses. If your entry is too late, you may lose the value of early identification and execution.

Your ideal strategy is to enter the field just before the adoption curve begins its steep rise. Using this strategy will allow you to escape the time and expense related to early development, while taking advantage of a rapidly growing market before competitors arise. Deciding when to make your move requires an understanding of market realities, a careful monitoring of developments, an adroit marketing strategy, and, often, a bit of luck! In general, it is better to be a little early than a little late.

The typical acceptance pattern of a new idea or approach is illustrated by the Fisher-Pry curve presented in Exhibit 7.1.

Exhibit 7.1. Fisher-Pry Curve

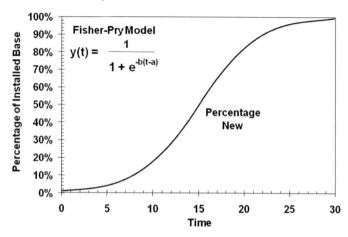

Source: Technology Futures, Inc.

For more information on Substitution Analysis and Fisher-Pry Analysis, see Technology Futures' article by Lawrence K. Vanston entitled "Practical Tips for Forecasting New Technology Adoption," http://www.tfi.com/minitrends/forecasting-tips.html.

Examine the potential implications of exogenous factors

The success or failure of any new enterprise is often determined by external factors over which the initiator has little or no control. Changing business cycles, new laws and regulations, technological breakthroughs, evolving tastes, unexpected events, and other developments only vaguely related to the Minitrend under consideration can impact its success or failure. Such factors may not only impact the final success of a Minitrend application, but may also affect the timing of this success.

Although the future is never completely predictable, many important developments cast long shadows before themselves. New advances in technologies are typically foreshadowed by discoveries in laboratories. Changing social attitudes are indicated by the formation of special interest groups. New laws and regulations are often suggested by political platforms and declared political positions.

In analyzing the potential success of a given Minitrend, you should look carefully at potential developments in the social, legal, regulatory, technological, financial, and other related arenas. You should also evaluate the potential impact of each of these developments on your Minitrend application—and what action might be taken to minimize negative developments and to take full advantage of positive developments. The wider your consideration of these exogenous factors, the less likely you will be blind-sided by unexpected events.

In Chapter Two, I note how the convergence of various technical and non-technical developments often provides very consequential outcomes. You should examine related developments that could support the successful exploitation of the trend in analyzing the application of a given Minitrend. The more possibilities of support involved, the greater the chance that your commitment to a Minitrend will be successful.

In the first chapter of the book, I note that Minitrends often manifest themselves as parts of larger Megatrends. In considering exogenous factors, you should give thought to other Minitrends that may be included in the relevant Megatrend. Taking a wide-angle view at this stage of the process may uncover new business opportunities or unexpected blindsiding threats.

EXAMINE THE OVERALL ATTRACTIVENESS OF THE MINITREND TO YOU PERSONALLY

Clarify your personal interests

Successful exploitation of any Minitrend will require a great amount of time and effort—and there is no guarantee that this effort will result in success. Concentrating your efforts on a single Minitrend, or a small group of related Minitrends, in which you have a personal interest is important. You should choose a Minitrend whose pursuit will provide you with a sense of involvement and satisfaction, one that piques your curiosity, and, if possible, one that can provide ancillary benefits such as relevance to your job.

Possible interests might be related to hobbies and pastimes, former occupations, interests of friends and relations, special assignments and training, involvement in social or professional associations, or consideration of a new career path.

The first step in determining whether a given Minitrend is "right for you" is to clarify, in your own mind, the areas that stir your imagination, conform with your education and experience, and coincide with your personal goals in life. Once you achieve this clarification, you can better judge how well a particular Minitrend matches your goals and desires.

Consider your personal situation

The primary purpose of your investment of time and effort in pursuing a particular Minitrend is to improve your personal situation in terms of income, position, recognition, self-satisfaction, security, and a host of other factors. How to best achieve these goals will depend in large measure on your particular situation.

If you are an individual or member of a small group of individuals who are seeking to initiate a new business venture, you have a great deal of freedom in selecting the Minitrend you wish to exploit. On the other hand, you probably have limited resources—time, funding, assistants, facilities—available to you. The Minitrends most attractive to you will probably be those characterized by low cost of entry, rapid market growth, and a reasonable probability of outside support.

If, on the other hand, you are exploring a commitment to a particular Minitrend as an employee of a company, the relative importance of the various factors may be different from those of an individual. Usually, a company will be willing to commit more resources, accept a longer pay-back period, and rely less on outside support than an individual. In general, the larger the company, the greater its willingness to accept these commitments will be.

COMPARE DIFFERENT MINITREND POSSIBILITIES

You will do better to concentrate on a single Minitrend or a small group of Minitrends rather than dissipating your effort among several trends at the same time. This does not mean that you shouldn't remain alert to new Minitrends as you do your analyses or that you might not shift your concentration to a new Minitrend if circumstances change.

If you find a number of Minitrends, or applications of Minitrends, particularly promising, then you must not only examine the attractiveness of each one individually, but must also compare their relative attractiveness. In making such a comparison, the factors to be considered are essentially those discussed in the previous paragraphs. In this case, however, you must also consider the relative importance of each of these factors to successful exploitation of the Minitrend, e.g., is timing more important than market size or is potential financial payoff less important than personal satisfaction?

Several years ago a large aerospace company became intrigued by a new business possibility. The demand for broader bandwidths for mobile communications was increasing rapidly, while the difficulty and cost of meeting this demand by conventional means was also growing. The company was considering the practicality of placing receiver/transmitters (transponders) at stratospheric altitudes to provide the demanded services. Such transponders would be able to serve much larger cones of reception than the network of individual towers currently in use. For example, a single transponder could serve a whole city the size of Atlanta, Chicago, or San Diego.

There were several approaches to placing transponders at these high altitudes and maintaining them there. For each approach, an existing company was positioned to provide the needed service. These approaches included:

— Manned Aircraft: Specially designed aircraft which would be rotated in space every eight hours.

— Unmanned Aircraft: Very light aircraft that would utilize solar cells to produce power and fuel cells for power storage. They would remain in place for a few months.

– Low-Altitude Airships: Relatively small airships (blimps) which would use solar power and be replaced every two or three months.

– High-Altitude Airships: Very large free flying airships (dirigibles) which would use solar power and remain in position for long periods of time, i.e., a year or more.

When Technology Futures was contracted to analyze the prospects, we began by identifying the factors to be considered: cost, potential revenue, coverage, culture, and company fit. We examined the advantages and disadvantages of each approach and came to the conclusion that the unmanned aircraft was the most promising short-term solution and the high-altitude airship was the best long-term solution.

We didn't believe, however, that any of the solutions would be commercially attractive in the following five years. Therefore, we recommended that the company not undertake any of the approaches at that time, and the company agreed with our recommendations. This was a Minitrend that didn't make the cut. However, with the growing interest in providing broadband service to rural areas in the United States, the project might justify reconsideration at this time.

In Chapter Two, I discuss the fact that very significant results often occur when correlated trends emerge simultaneously. In selecting the Minitrends to pursue, you may wish to investigate other trends—both technology-related and non-technology-related—that may increase the attractiveness of the Minitrend you are considering.

In our work helping individuals and organizations set up Minitrend projects, we find the Impact Wheel to be a quick, effective tool for assessing the marketplace consequences of external factors and for selecting a Minitrend for exploitation. Additional information on Impact Wheels may be found on the Minitrends website at http://www.minitrends.com/impact-wheels.

ALL VERY INTERESTING, BUT FRANKLY, SO WHAT?

In seeking to identify the Minitrend(s) you wish to exploit, you should first identify and make a preliminary analysis of a number of other potentially attractive trends. At some point, however, you must select the Minitrend(s) on which you wish to concentrate. The approaches described in this chapter can assist you in making that selection.

Once you have made the selection, you must then develop and execute a plan for exploitation. I discuss approaches for developing and implementing that plan in the next two chapters.

One further note: Early misanalysis, changing circumstances, or simple bad luck may materially reduce the attractiveness of the Minitrend that you have selected. Your plan should include checkpoints at which you can judge whether changes should be instituted or even if the project should be abandoned. This approach minimizes the possibility that you will continue to follow a dead-end path.

Chapter Eight

Developing a Minitrend Exploitation Scheme

T he development of a process to reap rewards, and the execution of that process, are the next steps in exploiting your chosen Minitrend. There are many excellent books that present the principles and processes of business planning. In essence, they all prescribe a three-step process:

- Define your current situation

- Decide where you want to be at some future time

- Determine how you are going to get from the current situation to the desired situation

Planning the exploitation of a Minitrend, however, is different. By definition, a Minitrend is still in the process of emerging. Therefore, deciding on your ultimate goal is difficult. Because of the uncertainties inherent in converting a Minitrend into a business success, I call the process a "Minitrend Exploitation Scheme," rather than a plan.

The principles governing the development of an exploitation scheme are similar whether the scheme is developed by individuals, small or medium-size companies, or large companies. However, the application of these principles varies with the group developing the scheme. Examining the characteristics of each group is useful in determining how the Minitrend can best be exploited.

CHARACTERISTICS OF GROUPS DEVELOPING THE EXPLOITATION SCHEME

Characteristics of individuals and small groups of individuals

Attributes: These people are anxious to make changes and advancements in their lives and willing to take risks to accomplish this. Typically, they are strong Type A personalities committed to personal and business success. These people tend to be quite risk-tolerant.

Goals: They seek to initially capture a small market segment and either grow with that segment or expand into other segments. They plan to eventually be acquired by a larger company, merge with a similar company, or initiate a public stock offering.

Resources: They are limited in terms of personnel, equipment, facilities, and funds and are capable of only limited product development and market research.

Timing: They need to gain market share rather quickly to remain viable.

Flexibility: They are generally capable of rapid adjustments when indicated, but need to be adroit in timing to take advantage of market developments.

Failure consequences: Often the individual(s) have to disband the project. Many of the people who disband one project later initiate another similar project. Individuals seeking to prosper from Minitrends tend to be aggressive, goal-driven, and willing to take significant risks to achieve their goals. The employment of Minitrends can be very useful in achieving their objectives.

Characteristics of small and medium-size companies

Attributes: These companies vary in terms of size, industry, business activities, and time in business. Generally, they have established product lines, customer bases, operating procedures, and knowledgeable employees. Because moving into new business lines will divert limited resources from current operations, these companies tend to be somewhat risk adverse.

Goals They seek to improve operations or to open new business lines.

Resources: They have sufficient personnel, equipment, facilities, and funds to support a fair amount of product development and market research.

Timing: They are able to wait a reasonable amount of time for markets to clarify.

Flexibility: They are generally able to make necessary changes to meet new market or technology realities.

Failure consequences: Failure may result in financial and other losses, but does not normally put the company's existence in jeopardy.

Small and medium-size companies must be continually alert to emerging Minitrends to protect themselves from competitors and to provide opportunities for business growth.

Characteristics of large companies

Attributes: These companies vary in terms of size, industry, business activities, and time in business. They have highly structured organizations, well-established product and service lines, long-term supplier and customer relationships, and a tendency to question innovation. This group tends to be somewhat risk adverse unless the scope of the commitment to a new business venture is small.

Goals: They seek to examine and, if justified, open new lines of business. Although Minitrends schemes may be developed internally, these companies tend to purchase other companies who have already completed the early stages of Minitrend exploitation.

Resources: They have sufficient personnel, equipment, facilities, and funds to support an extensive amount of product development and market research. The payoff from the exploitation of a Minitrend, however, must be sufficiently large to justify the movement of resources from ongoing operations.

Timing: They are able to wait a considerable length of time for markets to be proven and grow.

Flexibility: They are generally less able to react rapidly to changes in markets, procedures, or emerging opportunities than smaller companies.

Failure consequences: Failure may result in financial and other losses but does not normally cause major problems.

Minitrends can be particularly important to large companies because they have the resources to support their long-term development and to take full advantage of Minitrend successes.

DEVELOPING AN EFFECTIVE EXPLOITATION SCHEME

Developing an effective exploitation scheme involves a number of tasks, including the following:

- Defining the characteristics of the Minitrend you intend to exploit

- Analyzing the factors that support successful exploitation and those that inhibit this exploitation

- Preparing a series of alternate scenarios that provide a framework for exploitation

- Identifying the necessary tasks for accomplishing successful exploitation, who will be responsible for performing these tasks, and how these tasks can best be performed

Defining the Characteristics of the Minitrend

For the exploitation of a Minitrend, you need to determine how you can best utilize the special advantage offered by the trend. In most cases, there are a number of ways in which a given Minitrend can be utilized, and you must decide on which you will concentrate. The factors that you should examine include the following:

What are the domains that you will address?

There are many different industries, business arenas, companies, government agencies, academic institutions, non-profit organizations, and other groups that might be able to utilize the Minitrend effectively. Your task is to identify as many of these groups as possible and to evaluate the relative attractiveness of the Minitrend to each group. This analysis will serve as a basis for selecting a specific application of the Minitrend.

What is the nature of your application of the Minitrend?

For this analysis, you should determine whether your planned application will be a product, process, or procedure.

- **Product applications** are those that involve a product or service provided to customers (external or internal) in return for some type of recompense. Examples include consumer goods, software, component parts, delivery services, and maintenance.

- **Process applications** are those that involve the way a product is produced or a service is provided. Examples include improvements in manufacturing processes, internal distribution systems, and software programs.

- **Procedure applications** are those that involve the way in which products and processes are integrated into the operations of the organization. Examples include improvements in marketing methods, personnel policies, incentive programs, and external distribution systems.

The nature of the Minitrend applications presented in Chapter One can be classified as follows.

Products:

- The HAAN company's development of a steam mop
- American Superconductor's development of new equipment for wind energy
- Kurzweil Computer Products' development of a reading device for the blind

Processes:

- Michael Dell's reducing the costs of distributing computers by direct sales to customers

- YouTube's offering a vehicle to exchange film clips

- Pluck, Inc.'s utilizing proprietary software to help mainstream media outlets syndicate blog content

Procedures:

- Southwest Airlines' providing more dependable, economic, and friendly air travel service to customers

- Mobage Town's offering on-line games free of charge

- Swiss watch makers' changing marketing approach to appeal to the high-priced specialty market

- Bicycle manufacturers modifying their images to stress healthy and environmentally attractive devices, rather than low-cost transportation

From this review, you can see that there are attractive business opportunities in all three types of Minitrend applications. However, you will note that most of the Minitrends described in Chapters Four, Five, and Six are either Process or Procedure trends.

How great a change to the present situation will your Minitrend application cause?

- **Incremental changes** are those that reflect a relatively small improvement over present products, processes, and procedures. These advances are "a little better, a little faster, a little cheaper."

- **Distinctive changes** are those that provide significant advances or improvements, but are not based on fundamentally new technologies or approaches.

- **Breakthrough changes** are those based on fundamentally different technologies and approaches that allow the performance of functions that were previously not possible, or the performance of presently possible functions in a manner that is strikingly superior to the old.

Each of these types of change has advantages and disadvantages. Incremental changes typically require more limited resources and less time for exploitation and, thus, are often attractive to individuals and small companies. On the other hand, the gains from such changes are normally limited and timing is essential for success because competitors can move into the market more easily. Breakthrough changes are normally the aegis of large companies that have the resources to support an extended development period and to fully capitalize on a product's success.

Distinctive changes typically provide more attraction for customers than incremental changes, but do not require the time, effort, and funding necessary to bring breakthrough changes to maturity. In my experience, distinctive changes are normally the most appropriate Minitrend applications for both individuals and small and medium-size businesses.

What activities of targeted customer organizations will be affected by your Minitrend application?

- Will the application assist the organization's management to better define goals and objectives, to motivate desired actions by employees, to utilize resources more effectively, and/or to perform its basic functions more effectively?

- Will the application improve communications between the various elements of the organization and between the organization and its customers, clients, and suppliers?

- Will the application materially change for the better the infrastructure of the organization?

- Will the application provide incentives for employees to commit themselves to the achievement of the organization's goals and objectives?

- Will the application enhance sales and marketing activities?

An application that is useful in several of these activities will have a greater probability of success than one that is relevant to only one activity.

EMPLOYMENT OF ALTERNATE SCENARIO TECHNIQUES

Developing a set of alternate scenarios

In formulating business strategies and tactics, many organizations utilize some type of planning process in which the planners identify the objectives they hope to achieve, the tasks to be accomplished, the time required for each task, and the people responsible for accomplishing the tasks. The organizations integrate these elements to formulate a detailed business plan.

A well-considered Minitrend exploitation scheme includes many of the same elements as a business plan. A more flexible approach, however, is typically required to properly deal with the uncertainties inherent in the maturing of a Minitrend. In this environment, an "alternate scenario" approach is usually more effective.

A "scenario" is a coordinated set of assumptions about how the future may develop used to assist in organizational planning. In an alternate scenario approach, a set of scenarios is developed, each of which describes a different feasible "future." A scheme is then developed to address each of these futures. Finally, these schemes are integrated into a composite exploitation scheme with sufficient flexibility to react to changes in business and operating environments. Such a set of alternate scenarios normally include a Base Scenario that reflects the assumptions deemed to be most probable, and a small number of Divergent Scenarios that reflect different sets of feasible assumptions.

The first step in developing a set of alternate scenarios is to define the overall areas to be included in the scenarios. These areas should be very broad in scope, e.g., the economy, international relations, demography, government policy, technology advances, education structures, and societal issues. The purpose of this step is to insure that you are not overlooking issues that might materially impact the success of your Mini-trend application. These areas will vary among Mini-trends depending on circumstance. For example, company policy, although not as broad as some of the others mentioned, will be an important area of interest for an established company, but not for a start-up enterprise.

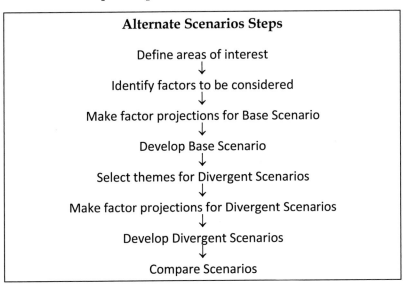

Alternate Scenarios Steps

Define areas of interest
↓
Identify factors to be considered
↓
Make factor projections for Base Scenario
↓
Develop Base Scenario
↓
Select themes for Divergent Scenarios
↓
Make factor projections for Divergent Scenarios
↓
Develop Divergent Scenarios
↓
Compare Scenarios

Identify factors to be considered

In this step, you select the most relevant factors within each area of interest. These factors will be less general than the areas of interest and more focused on the success of the Mini-trend application. Within the government policy area, for example, relevant factors might be regulations, tax policies, and government incentives. Within the demographics area, factors might include the number of people in each age cohort, racial, ethnic, and gender balances, and geographic distribution. Within the education area, factors might include federal government assistance, number of teachers in elementary schools, extent of home schooling, and new building investments. Because of resource limitations, the number of factors considered is normally limited to those of greatest importance to the application. My experience is that for a fairly large alternate scenario project, somewhere between twenty and forty factors can reasonably be considered.

Make factor projections for Base Scenario

Your next step is to project how the selected factors will most probably change in the future. At this point, these projections will be completed independently. How far into the future these factors are to be projected will depend on the scope of the exploitation scheme. In general, the projections should extend about twice the time horizon of the scheme.

Develop Base Scenario

For this step you need to combine the projections for the individual factors into an overall forecast, i.e. the Base Scenario, that represents your view of how the future will most likely transpire.

Select themes for Divergent Scenarios

Now you must select themes for the Divergent Scenarios that you plan to develop. These themes provide a basis for identifying future developments that could materially impact, for better or worse, the success or failures of your application. Examples might include increased or decreased demand for your application, emergence of an attractive competitive product or service, an economic downturn or upturn, changes in political realities, changes in international relationships, etc. Normally, availability of resources restrict the number of Divergent Scenarios to a small number, i.e., three to five.

Many organizations commonly prepare three scenarios— good news, bad news, and intermediate news. My experience is that these choices are seldom of much value because planners tend to only seriously consider the medium scenario and mostly ignore the other two. Moreover, overall situations are not normally all good or all bad. It is preferable to select themes that are reasonably plausible, but which will cause significantly different actions by the organization.

Make factor projections for Divergent Scenarios

This step is similar to the one described for the Base Scenario except the projections will be influenced by the specific theme. For example, an increase in federal government aid to schools will undoubtedly impact the number of elementary school teachers.

Develop Divergent Scenarios

As in the case of the Base Scenario, you must integrate the factor projections into each of the Divergent Scenarios. The development of a set of alternate scenarios involves a commitment of time, effort, and funding. Therefore, the number of themes considered, the number of factors addressed, the amount of detail included in each scenario, and the time frames considered will depend on the resources available. However, even individuals and small companies are usually capable of developing at least a limited scenario set. In general, the larger the organization developing the scenarios, the more effort can be expended on this task.

In 1982, the U.S. National Science Foundation (NSF) contracted Technology Futures, Inc. (TFI) to assist it in developing an Electric Power Policy for the nation. To accomplish this task, we decided to utilize an alternate scenario approach. The Base Scenario reflected our projections until the Year 2010 of 28 different factors, including total energy use, gross domestic product, population growth and distribution, oil prices, and similar factors. The themes selected for divergent scenarios were: (1) nuclear resurgence, (2) a "post industrial" economic structure, (3) increased reliance on coal plants, (4) economic malaise, (5) major increase in economic activity, and (6) distinctive new energy sources, e.g., fusion power, solar collectors in space, and breeder nuclear reactors. Projections were then developed for the 28 factors under each theme, and divergent scenarios were formulated for each theme. These scenarios were then used to develop recommendations for the NSF.

This project involved six TFI employees, an advisory board of twelve experts in various relevant areas, and 125 participants in various surveys and interviews. Techniques utilized for factor projections included Trend Analyses, Fisher-Pry Analysis, Gompertz Curves,

Analogy Analysis, Impact Wheels, Nominal Group Conferencing, and Delphi Surveys.

A comparison of some of the more important 1982 projections for the Year 2010 and the situation in the Year 2007 is presented in the table below. It will be noted that, with the exception of Population, all of the listed factors are within the ranges projected in the scenarios, and most are close to those projected in the base scenario.

NSF Projections

Factor	Base Scenario Projection (2010)	Range of Projections (2010)	Actual (2007)
RGNP (billion 1980$)	$5,050	$4,110–$6,400	$4,700
Population Size	275 million	275–290 million	300 million
Energy Demand (quadrillion BTU)	100	80–130	100
Net Electricity Demand (billion kwh)	2,381	2,381–6,825	2,808

The procedures used in this project, together with the results, are described in the book, *Principles for Electric Power Policy*, Quorum Press, 1984.

Characteristics of a useful scenario set

In order to be useful in the developing the exploitation scheme, the scenario set should include the following characteristics.

- **Be Plausible:** Although, by definition, the divergent scenarios are not those that the developer or those using the scenarios believe are most probable, they must be recognized as feasible by the target audience.

In a study conducted by TFI for the National Aeronautics and Space Administration (NASA), we examined the possible use of non-fossil fuels to power aircraft. As part of this project, we developed six scenarios. We then conducted a meeting with a number of business, military, government, and other leaders to examine the implications of each of these scenarios in regard to possible fuels.

One of the themes we selected for a divergent scenario was "Economic Malaise." This scenario included a projection that the unemployment rate in the United States would reach six percent within the next five years. One participant, the Director of Research for the United Automobile Workers Union, insisted that this projection was impossible because if the country ever reached this level of unemployment, there would be a revolution. To gain his agreement to continue in the project we reduced this figure to five percent

Four months later the unemployment rate exceeded seven percent. This example illustrates that acceptance of a given scenario depends on the user's perception of feasibility, not on actual feasibility.

- **Be Self-Consistent:** In formulating scenarios, each factor is projected independently. This can lead to inconsistencies between factors. For example, if the projected rate of population growth is inconsistent with the projected immigration rate, this inconsistency must be resolved. Therefore, you must be careful to review scenarios to eliminate such inconsistencies.

- **Be Somewhat Bounding:** Because of the effort involved in developing and analyzing scenarios, you are limited in the number of scenarios that you can practically employ—usually three to five. Since your goal is to provide an "envelope" of possible futures, you must choose your themes carefully. A reasonable rule-of-thumb is that each divergent scenario should be sufficiently different from the base scenario that it would cause the organization to adopt a different exploitation scheme.

- **Include Critical Factors:** Since including all possible factors that might impact the success of the Minitrend application is impractical, you must identify the most important ones to include in the scenario set.

Advantages of an alternate scenario approach

Forces flexible planning

The formulation of alternate scenarios forces planners to recognize the uncertainty of the future and to realize that the assumptions embedded in the exploitation scheme may prove to be wrong. By identifying and evaluating these uncertainties, the planner is more likely to give consideration to these uncertainties and, thus, add flexibility to the scheme. This flexibility is particularly important in Minitrend planning because the Minitrend is, by definition, still in an emerging state.

Provides a basis for a monitoring plan

The proposed exploitation scheme will develop in an environment subject to many changes. Continued monitoring of those factors that will significantly impact your Minitrend application is very important. However, monitoring all of the factors will be very difficult. The alternate scenario approach helps to identify the factors of greatest importance and can provide a basis for tailoring an effective monitoring plan.

Aids intra-organization communication

People throughout the organization must provide information and insight for the alternate scenario approach to be most effective. This input not only improves the quality of the scenarios, but also gets these individuals involved in the planning process and dedicated to its success.

Encourages imaginative thinking

Because the formulation of alternate scenarios has a strong "what if" quality, the process often elicits ideas and observations that are discouraged in a normal planning process. In this atmosphere, imaginative thinking is acknowledged, appreciated, and promoted. An individual who, in a traditional planning process, would be "that person with the weird ideas" becomes an "out-of-the-box thinker" in an alternate scenario process.

Identifies future decisions

A basic premise of the alternate scenario approach is that the original exploitation scheme may be modified if the operating environment changes, i.e., if one of the Divergent Scenarios appears to be evolving rather than the Base Scenario. By identifying and defining possible Divergent Scenarios, you will be able to define key decision points and be forewarned of decisions that may be required in the future.

Benefiting from flexibility

The basic purpose of utilizing the alternate scenario approach is to add flexibility to exploitation scheme. To achieve this flexibility, you must be constantly alert to changes in the controlling factors. In formulating the alternate scenarios, you will have identified those factors most important to the success of your Minitrend application. Important changes will be easier to recognize. However, this requires constant monitoring of changes, as well as appropriate modifications of the exploitation scheme.

IDENTIFYING THE NECESSARY TASKS

Once you formulate your set of alternate scenarios, utilizing them in developing your exploitation scheme is the next step. The scenarios are not a substitute for a scheme, but rather, describe environments in which the scheme can be developed and executed. The traditional steps in the planning process—clarifying objectives, analyzing markets, assessing available resources, identifying required tasks, assigning responsibilities, etc.—must still be taken. You now, however, have a milieu in which to develop your exploitation scheme.

Because developing business plans is not a major objective of this book, I do not go into details about the planning process. However, there are a number of excellent resources available describing the traditional planning process. These include:

- Friend, Graham and Zehle, Stefan. 2009. *Guide to Business Planning (Economist Books)*. Bloomberg Press. This guide covers a wide range of business planning subjects, including market analysis, financial planning, and contingency planning. It is part of the *Economist* magazine's business management series.

- Gevurtz, Franklin A. 2008. *Gevurtz's Business Planning: Cases and Materials*. Foundation Press. This book presents a number of cases related to business activities with an emphasis on legal aspects. It is part of the *University Casebook Series*.

- Bangs, David H. 2002. *The Business Planning Guide: Creating a Plan for Success in Your Own Business (Eighth Edition)*. Dearborn Press. This book addresses all aspects of business planning, including the elements to be included, suggestions for putting the plan into action, and how to present the plan to potential funding sources. It is aimed primarily for start-up businesses.

ALL VERY INTERESTING, BUT FRANKLY, SO WHAT?

In previous chapters, I discuss the benefits of recognizing and exploiting Minitrends; I present techniques for identifying and evaluating promising Minitrends; I list a number of Minitrends that I believe will be of significant importance in the near future; and I give advice on selecting a Minitrend or Minitrends for exploitation. In this chapter, I offer some suggestions for exploiting Minitrends.

In each of these chapters I state my belief that formulating an exploitation scheme can be interesting, may open new avenues of adventure, and may be a source of personal satisfaction. However, as you perform the indicated actions, you must keep in mind that *the primary purpose of your Minitrend activities is to make money.*

In order to meet this objective, you must define the market that you intend to serve, determine what will appeal to this market, clarify how your selected Minitrend application can serve this market, and plan how you can successfully match your Minitrend application to market needs. Because your Minitrend will be in the emerging phase, its market may be volatile and difficult to define. You must be continually alert to market changes and quick to modify your exploitation scheme to meet these changes. Flexibility of mindset, objectives, and actions are hallmarks of successful Minitrend exploitation.

Another important aspect of Minitrend exploitation is timing. Entry into the market too early, i.e., before the Minitrend has sufficiently emerged, can lead to misapplication of time, effort, and funds. On the other hand, entry into the market too late—that is after the Minitrend is widely recognized and its value appreciated—can dissipate the advantages of early identification. Again, timing and flexibility go hand-in-hand with successful Minitrend exploitation.

In the following chapter, I present some suggestions on how you can successfully execute Minitrend exploitation schemes.

Chapter Nine

Putting the Exploitation Scheme into Action

As discussed in the last chapter, developing a well-conceived Minitrend exploitation scheme is a significant step in the Minitrend process. Once you accomplish this, you are ready for the most important step: translating your scheme into a successful business enterprise.

Keep in mind the nature of this task: you are seeking to find ways to take advantage of a specific situation in which you have a special perceptiveness. Tailoring your approach to fit your particular situation is essential. Your specific approach will be quite different if you are an individual planning on starting a new business, an executive of a small or medium-size business looking for a new product line or a new way to improve the company's operations, or an employee of a large established company that is looking for an attractive merger or acquisition. Regardless of your particular situation, however, what you are seeking to determine are ways to take advantage of both your unique vision *and* the unique ways in which you translate that vision into a successful business application.

I suggest these actions to assist you in this translation:

IDENTIFY MARKET NEEDS

The most important single factor driving the success of your Minitrend application will be a market need for the application. By this point, you should have formed a good idea of the need from the analyses that you conducted to identify and select the Minitrend in question. The basic questions in defining market needs are:

- Can anyone make money from the application, and, if so, who are they and how much money can they make?

- Can anyone save money from the application, and, if so, who are they and how much money can they save?

- Will the application solve anyone's problems, and, if so, what are the problems and who can be helped?

- Will the application provide anyone personal satisfaction, and, if so, who and how?

Standard market analysis techniques can assist in answering these questions. There is, however, one caveat. Although common wisdom is that you must respond to customers' needs and desires, my experience has been that, when asked what they would like to have, almost all customers, regardless of company, industry, or region, ask for the same thing. They ask for something that is very much like what they currently use, but a little better, a little cheaper, a little faster, a little more efficient. The key to real product success is determining what would truly delight the customer, but which the customer does not know to ask for. By their basic nature, Minitrends often provide new ideas and approaches that can satisfy these undefined needs and desires.

DETERMINE THE SPECIAL FEATURES OF THE MINITREND

When you selected the Minitrend you plan to exploit, there were undoubtedly some characteristics that spurred your interest. In your efforts to execute your exploitation scheme, you should clarify in your own mind what the special features of the Minitrend are. Then you should examine why and how these features will be attractive to each of your potential clients. To be successful, the new enterprise must have some special attractiveness to particular customers or clients.

Personal conversations, questionnaires, surveys, and structured or unstructured meetings are all excellent tools for clarifying the needs and desires of your potential customers. This can be invaluable in determining how your product can satisfy these needs and desires. (A number of companies have utilized the virtual world platforms discussed in Chapter Four to test the market potential of new products and services.) You should remember that clients often don't recognize, or at least don't express, a desire for those products and services that would truly delight them if they were available.

CONVINCE POTENTIAL CUSTOMERS OF THE VALUE OF THE MINITREND'S SPECIAL FEATURES

To successfully execute your exploitation scheme, you must convince potential customers of the unique value of the new product or service to them, their companies, or their customers and clients. To assist in this task, you should remember that a simple working model is always better than the best verbal description in the world.

Remembering that many decisions are, in large measure, based on emotions is also important. Most people like to think of themselves as being logical human beings, but in reality, value-laden factors often determine their decisions. For example, as I mentioned in Chapter One, the primary reason for the original success of Starbucks is not that the coffee itself is markedly superior to the much cheaper coffee at McDonalds. The primary reason customers choose Starbucks is that it provides an opportunity for customers to pamper themselves in a relaxed and friendly atmosphere.

You should, therefore, give careful thought to customers' old habits that must be modified before your new product or service will be accepted. In many cases, customers must be convinced to overcome well-established prejudices, many of which are basically emotional.

In practice, the importance of emotion in decision-making can serve as an advantage in the exploitation of a Minitrend. By their nature, Minitrends often inspire interest and excitement.

CAREFULLY CONSIDER HOW YOUR PRODUCT OR SERVICE WILL BE MARKETED

There are many factors you must consider when determining how your new product or service can best be marketed. These factors include the nature of the product, the nature of the market to be addressed, the timing of product introduction, communication tools to be employed, and market stratification.

The success of the product depends on whether it provides a financial benefit to a customer, solves or prevents an important customer problem, or promotes emotional satisfaction for the customer. The successful initiator must give careful consideration to which of these attractions is best served by the product or service. Examining successful similar products is often useful in designing a marketing program.

Timing may be particularly important to success. The perfect time to introduce the product is when its introduction coincides with the emergence of a perceived need.

Sometimes, offering a unique or special enticement to promote a new product or service can be useful, especially if a strong competitor is already in the field. Although the founders of Southwest Airlines recognized the value of frequent, low-cost air service for business passengers in Texas, they also understood the special appeal of free liquor for passengers. (At one time Southwest Airlines was the largest distributor of hard liquor in the State of Texas.)

LOOK FOR OPPORTUNITIES TO TAKE ADVANTAGE OF CONVERGENCES

As I discussed in Chapter Two, there are numerous historic examples in which simultaneous developments in two different technologies or a combination of a technical advance and a new non-technical development have resulted in significant new business opportunities. You should, therefore, search for other Minitrends that might positively impact your probability of success when executing your exploitations scheme. Often, such related Minitrends will be included in the

Megatrend of which your Minitrend is a part. The convergent trends may be technical, non-technical, or a combination of both.

CAREFULLY DEFINE AND EVALUATE RELEVANT DRIVERS AND CONSTRAINTS

The success of a new enterprise will depend on exogenous factors over which the initiator has little or no control. You should examine these factors and determine how to take fullest advantage of the positive factors and minimize the ill effects of the negative ones.

Often there are basic drivers that increase the probability of exploitation scheme success. Such drivers include:

- Pent up demand for a product or service with the characteristics of the Minitrend

- Increasing awareness of advantages offered by the Minitrend in the commercial arena and among the general public

- The emergence of supporting ideas and approaches

- Unexpected advances in Minitrend technology

- New governmental laws and regulations

- Media attention

Just as the success of your exploitation scheme can be supported by drivers, that success can be jeopardized by various constraints. Such constraints include:

- The emergence of other approaches that provide the same or similar advantages

- Unacceptable costs or difficulties in employing the application

- The existence of important individuals or organizations that will lose money or prestige if the application is successful

- A demonstrated failure of the application or similar application

- The natural hesitancy of some individuals and organizations to accept new ideas or approaches

Once the drivers and constraints are defined, you must consider:

- How important each is to the success of the enterprise?

- What individuals or organizations will play a significant role in enterprise success or failure?

- What is the true balance between drivers and constraints?

- Perhaps most important, what can you do to swing that balance in your favor?

When you have identified and analyzed the drivers and constraints to your exploitation scheme, you can define the actions needed to gain maximum advantage from drivers and minimize the impact of the constraints.

EXAMINE ANALOGOUS SITUATIONS

Typically, individuals and organizations respond to similar circumstances in similar manners. By examining the experiences of similar enterprises, you can get a better picture of the process of development and adoption. For example, if you had wished to project the adoption of high definition television, you might well have examined the adoption of color television. If you had wished to project the adoption of color television, you might have examined the adoption of black and white television. If you had wished to project the adoption of black and white television, you might have examined the adoption of commercial radio.

In examining the adoption patterns of past new enterprises, however, you must remember that, because of a number of factors including the revolution in communications technologies such as Facebook, PayPal, YouTube, MySpace, and other

Web 2.0 offerings, the pattern of new enterprise development is often much faster than it has been in the past.

Most people are impressed with success. The success of your exploitation scheme can be enhanced by a previous success of similar Minitrend exploitations or by a success of the same type of exploitation in a different arena. Success breeds success!

ENGAGE ALLIES AND SUPPORTERS

Often there are other individuals or organizations that will profit from the introduction and acceptance of your Minitrend application. These individuals and organizations may be willing and able to assist in the successful execution of your exploitation scheme. This assistance may be in the form a providing financial support, introducing you to other interested parties, or suggesting improvements to your scheme.

BE FLEXIBLE

By definition, Minitrends are not yet fully developed. That the trends will take unexpected twists and turns is not only possible, but probable. You must be alert to changes in the nature, timing, and/or implications of the trend. This requires continuous monitoring of the forces that could impact the development of the trend. As indicated in Chapter Eight, the formulation of a set of alternate scenarios can assist you in focusing your monitoring efforts and assist you in reacting quickly to changes in the operating environment.

An example of the value of flexibility is provided by the actions of Dr. Richard Sandor, a research professor at the Kellogg Graduate School of Management at Northwestern University. In 2003, in order to project the adoption of trade in carbon emission credits in the United States, Dr. Sandor launched the Chicago Climate Exchange (CCX). When the United States failed to approve the Kyoto Protocol on carbon emissions, there appeared to be little incentive for a "cap and trade" structure in the U.S. However, Mr. Sandor then established the European Climate Exchange where European companies can buy and sell permission to emit carbon dioxide into the atmosphere. This exchange has had remarkable business success. Moreover, CCX is now well situated to profit significantly if the United States adopts a cap and trade system in the future.

REMEMBER THERE ARE OTHER SMART PEOPLE IN THE WORLD

You will not, unfortunately, be allowed to execute your exploitation scheme in a vacuum. The primary value of Minitrends is that most people and organizations are either not aware of the trends or fail to appreciate their implications. In the real world, there are usually other individuals who may also recognize the business opportunities afforded by the trends. You must give serious consideration to potential competitors.

In doing effective competitor analysis, you must consider:

- What are competitors capable of doing?

- What are they likely to do?

- What you can do to address potential competitor actions?

Examining the nature of potential competition is also useful. Competitors can be basically classified into three categories:

- **Direct Competitors,** who will offer the same or similar products or services

- **Indirect Competitors,** who will offer a different product that provides the same or similar function

- **Structural Competitors,** who will eliminate or drastically reduce the need for the product

Delta Airlines is a direct competitor to American Airlines; railroads, buses, and passenger cars are indirect competitors of American Airlines; and teleconferencing is a structural competitor to American Airlines. In reality, most organizations pay close attention to direct competitors; give at least cursory attention to indirect competitors; and give little heed to structural competitors who are often the ones who provide the greatest threats to continuing success.

STAY HEALTHY

Several years ago, Dr. Karl Vesper, a faculty member of the University of Washington's Engineering College and Business College and a leading authority of entrepreneurship, reviewed a number of studies on the characteristics of successful entrepreneurs. In this review he noted that the most common characteristic of these people was not initiative, drive, imagination, or the other qualities generally associated with such people, but rather exceptionally good health. Dr. Vesper couldn't determine whether this indicated that only healthy individuals were motivated to undertake new business challenges; whether only healthy individuals were able to withstand the stress and strains associated with entrepreneurship; whether involvement in entrepreneurial activities kept individuals healthy; or whether individuals involved in entrepreneurial activities simply didn't have time to be unhealthy.

Regardless of the reason for this reality, it does appear important that individuals embarking on such challenging endeavors maintain their personal health. I advise you to maintain an active exercise program, follow a reasonable diet, keep weight down, avoid smoking, and engage in at least some recreational activity. You should probably also keep reasonable working hours, although this is not a common practice among entrepreneurs.

> The founder of an Austin, Texas, software company declared publicly that in his organization, both he and his fellow managers worked only forty-hour weeks, which kept them imaginative and alert. Ironically, what he did not say was that his programmers typically worked fourteen-hour days, seven days a week.

ALWAYS APPLY A "SANITY TEST" AT EACH STAGE OF THE EXPLOITATION PROCESS

There is an old saying that if something seems too good to be true, then it probably is. Often people involved in exploiting a Minitrend become overly enamored with their enterprise and fail to examine some of their assumptions with a clear eye. Although optimism is normally a required attribute for a successful project initiator, blind optimism can lead to enterprise failure. Initiators must constantly review their assumptions to determine if they are currently valid and if they will remain valid in the future.

In addition to their own evaluation of current and future realities, I advise initiators to utilize the experience, insights, and wisdom of others. A number of studies have shown that the combined views of several experts are more valid than the views of any single expert. There are tools available to assist in gathering the views of others, e.g., Impact Wheels, Stakeholder Analysis, Nominal Group Conferencing, and Delphi Surveys. Of course, sometimes the initiator must "go with his or her gut." This should be done, however, only after the opinions of others have been considered.

Although there are formal methods for evaluating the business potential of new enterprises, you can often deduce a great deal by simply asking yourself if "it just feels right" or if "it just doesn't feel right." Often our subconscious gives us important insights that we really can't explain.

For more information on forecasting methodologies, see my article on the Technology Futures, Inc. website entitled "Better Forecasts, Better Plans, Better Results," http://www.tfi.com/minitrends/better-forecasts.html. More details on Impact Wheels may be found on the Minitrends site at http://www.minitrends.com/impact-wheels.

ALL VERY INTERESTING, BUT FRANKLY, SO WHAT?

So now you have shown yourself alert enough to recognize promising Minitrends, clever enough to appreciate their significance, and talented enough to take full advantage of the opportunities that they represent. You have used the suggestions that I present in this book to identify some particularly attractive Minitrends. You have selected the Minitrend on which to concentrate your attention. You have developed a dynamic exploitation scheme, and you are well on the way to successfully executing that scheme.

In accomplishing these tasks you have benefited financially and/or improved your standing in your company or organization. You are pleased at your success, and you have every reason to be proud.

By being one of the first, or perhaps the first, to take full advantage of the Minitrend, you are now in a position to dominate the field and to establish the rules of the game. You have the advantage of widespread brand recognition and may even receive generic recognition for your product as was the case with Kleenex, Cellophane, and Band-Aids.

The game, however, isn't over. Your very success has enhanced the recognition and appreciation of the Minitrend involved, so you face increasing competition. Although patent and copyright laws provide you a certain amount of protection, there are usually a number of ways these laws can be evaded. In the real world, keeping others from taking away your toys is very difficult. Your best approach is to develop new toys.

This principle is borne out by the actions of Reed Hastings, CEO of Netflix, described in Chapter Two. The company has been a phenomenal success. Noting the decreasing demand for DVD rentals, however, Netflix now offers subscribers the choice of streaming videos directly to their PCs from the company's website. This simplifies ordering movies, eliminates mail delivery delays, and reduces the cost of delivering the service from the current eighty cents to about a nickel.

About four out of every five new enterprises fail in the first five years of existence. I believe that one of the major reasons for such a high failure rate is that the company leadership doesn't dedicate itself to continually updating its products and services and the ways it provides them. The recognition and exploitation of emerging Minitrends is a solid approach to achieving such updating.

The problem of protecting your turf is eliminated if, despite your best efforts, your exploitation project doesn't succeed. In that case, in the words of a popular song, you should "pick yourself up, brush yourself off, and start all over again." There are, of course, lots of Minitrends in the sea. There are a vast number of cases in which an individual has failed at one enterprise only to succeed at another. If necessary, there is no reason why you shouldn't add yourself to this list.

Before you begin exploitation of another Minitrend, you should examine why your previous attempt didn't succeed. Secretary of Defense Robert Gates defines experience as the ability to recognize your mistakes when you make them— again. Hopefully, if you don't succeed in your first endeavor, you will not make the same mistakes—again.

Chapter Ten

Here's the *So What!*

A t the end of each of the first nine chapters of this book, I sum up what I believe to be the basic wisdom of that chapter. However, each of the subjects is presented separately. In reality, the real value of the Minitrend concept is the melding of all of these individual subjects.

In the process of "Following the Money" or "Following the Leaders," you not only identify emerging trends, but you also get a preliminary idea of potential business opportunities associated with them. In the process of "Looking for Convergences," you begin to consider which Minitrends may be interrelated. In the process of defining the overall attractiveness of a Minitrend to the business community and to yourself, you not only select the Minitrends to be exploited, but also gain insights on how that exploitation can be achieved. In short, as explained in Chapter One, applying the Minitrends concept is not a step-by-step process, but rather the adoption of a mindset that encompasses all of the elements of the concept.

This mindset will open your imagination, your creativity, and your curiosity. Your ability to make the most of your circumstances and to distinguish yourself from colleagues, compatriots, and competitors will be enhanced. You will also find you have a heightened alertness and awareness of promising Minitrends as the world unfolds around you—and you will begin to recognize business opportunities that arise from such Minitrends. Minitrend followers are dreamers looking for adventure, and commitment to the concept can make the adventure intriguing, exciting, and lucrative. As you continue on your Minitrend Adventure, you will identify an enormous number of interesting Minitrends.

For more than thirty years, I have assisted companies, government agencies, and academic institutions in conducting technology forecasts. In these forecasts, we always had to consider not only the technical aspects of the technology, but also the market, regulatory, economic, and social trends that would affect, and be affected by, advances in the technology. As I became more familiar with the Minitrend concept, it became increasingly obvious that technology forecasting and Minitrend analysis go hand-in-hand. Thus, launching into the Minitrend Adventure was a natural extension of my experience in technology forecasting.

When I began work on this book, I found myself immersed in a tide of interesting Minitrends. These trends involved many arenas—technical, social, political, economic, demographic, and a host of others.

I was not able to make more than a cursory examination of the many interesting Minitrends that I uncovered, much less develop them into business applications. However, several of the Minitrends I analyzed have assisted me and my company, Technology Futures, Inc., in our business planning and in converting these plans into actions. In the "Minitrends and small and medium-size companies" section of Chapter One, I describe the positive long-term role that Minitrends have played in the continuing success of our company. In addition to the business value of applying the Minitrends concept, just being alert to these emerging trends has added interest to my life. I am confident that you will experience the same phenomenon if you commit yourself to a Minitrend Adventure.

ಞ ಜಿ

The famed mythologist Joseph Campbell encouraged his followers to "Follow your Bliss." He wrote, "If you follow your bliss, you put yourself on a kind of track that has been there all the while, waiting for you, and the life that you ought to be living is the one you are living."

I hope that embarking on a Minitrend Adventure will assist you in following your own bliss.

Index

JOHN H. VANSTON, PH.D.
Chairman
Technology Futures, Inc.

Dr. John Vanston is an internationally-renowned consultant, educator, speaker, and award-winning author in the fields of technology forecasting, technology/market integration, trend analysis, and technology management in uncertain environments.

He founded Technology Futures, Inc. (TFI) in 1978, building the Austin, Texas, company into a leading authority in custom research, forecasting, and trend analysis in telecom and other high-technology industries.

At TFI, John has conducted analyses of emerging technologies for a wide range of commercial, government, and academic organizations. These analyses have assisted his business clients in gaining sustainable competitive advantage and provided his government clients with important new information, insights, and advice that have increased the effectiveness of their operations

Prior to establishing TFI, John served as a professor of nuclear engineering at the University of Texas at Austin and as the deputy director of the University's Center for Energy Studies. While at the University, he conducted a number of forecasts and trend analyses in the energy area. Earlier, John served as a Lieutenant Colonel in the U.S. Army.

CARRIE VANSTON
Media and Marketing Director
Technology Futures, Inc.

Book collaborator Carrie Vanston has many years of experience in public relations, marketing, and sales at Technology Futures, Inc. and in the entertainment industry. Because the successful exploitation of a Minitrend requires effective marketing, she brings a distinct real-world quality to the book, particularly in the media communications and social media areas. Her easy sense of style and readability helps the reader to connect with the Minitrends concept.